What Went Wrong with Mr. Right

Other books by Ann Gadd
(published by Findhorn Press)

The Girl Who Bites Her Nails and the Man Who Is Always Late:
What Our Habits Reveal About Us

The A–Z Guide to Common Habits: Overcoming Them Through Affirmations

Climbing the Beanstalk: The Hidden Messages Found in Best-Loved Fairy Tales

Finding Your Feet: How the Sole Reflects the Soul

PEFC

PEFC - 16-33-250

This book is printed on paper that
includes a minimum of 70 % of PEFC
certified material from forest which
has been certified against a PEFC
endorsed forest certification scheme
as sustainably managed.
www.pefc.org

What Went Wrong With Mr. Right

Why relationships fail and how to heal them

by
Ann Gadd

FINDHORN PRESS

© Ann Gadd 2009

The right of Ann Gadd to be identified as the author of this work
has been asserted by her in accordance with the
Copyright, Designs and Patents Act 1998.

First published by Findhorn Press 2009

ISBN: 978-1-84409-154-6

British Library Cataloguing-in-Publication Data.
A catalogue record for this book is available from the British Library.

Edited by Michael Hawkins
Cover design by Damian Keenan
Layout by Prepress-Solutions.com
Printed and bound in the European Union

1 2 3 4 5 6 7 8 9 10 11 12 13 14 13 12 11 10 09

Published by
Findhorn Press
305A The Park,
Findhorn, Forres
Scotland IV36 3TE

Tel +44(0)1309 690582
Fax +44(0)131 777 2711
eMail info@findhornpress.com
www.findhornpress.com

Dedication

To Anthony
For being the mirror to my soul

Acknowledgements

No book gets written in isolation.

For those of you who read through the draft, Anne, Gareth, Glyn, Jane, Jenny, Lydia and especially Michael Hawkins, the editor, whose feedback has made this a better book; for those of you whose stories are woven into its fabric and for those fellow travellers, both friend and ostensibly foe who have been my mirror, my deepest heartfelt thanks.

But what if I should discover that the least among them all, the poorest of all the beggars, the most impudent of all the offenders, the very enemy himself – that these are within me, and that I myself stand in need of the alms of my own kindness, that I myself am the enemy who must be loved – what then?[1]

—Carl Jung

[1] *Psychology and Religion: East and West* (New York: Pantheon, 1958), p. 339.www.criticalvision.
blogspot.com/2006/03/carl-jung-on-selves-and-shadows.html - 46k

Table of Contents

Introduction

Man is neither angel nor beast; and the misfortune is that he who would act the angel acts the beast.[2]

–Blaise Pascal (1632-1662)
French scientific and philosophical genius

"I enjoy fighting. I know it sounds weird, but I deliberately go round looking for an opportunity to beat someone up. Even as a teenager I used to thrive on a good punch-up. When things weren't going well at home, thumping some bloke in a rugby match felt like a huge release for me. I deliberately tried to hurt my opponents. Later, I moved to pubs and clubs, where I would try and pick a fight. More recently, I've started doing road rage as a way of expressing my anger."

The man sitting opposite me fidgeted uncomfortably in the chair that seemed too small to contain his large, muscled frame. The chair had become a source of restriction for him – a sort of cage and he seemed to be fighting a compulsion to get up and leave. He clearly felt very awkward in this situation.

As we talked, he did express some remorse about his past behaviour, acknowledging that it had caused hurt to others, yet his anger possessed him to the extent that it controlled him and he blamed this as the reason for his violent outbursts.

It began, he recalled, when in his early teenage years, his parents went through a traumatic divorce. Unable to express the emotions that raged within him verbally, he took these feelings onto the sports field, where, being bigger than most of his team, he found release in aggressive play. This became the only way he knew of working through the emotions he felt unable to express.

He is a type A- personality: "I constantly live in fear of the future which keeps me on the go, protecting my interests. It's like , if I stopped for one moment from being busy, I would lose my guard and things would go pear-shaped." It did not come as a

---

[2] P. 99, l. 4. (358) Project Gutenberg *Man is neither angel nor brute*, etc.— Montaigne, *Essais*, iii, 13.The Project Gutenberg EBook of Pascal's Pensées, by Blaise Pascal

surprise then to discover that he suffered from high blood pressure. As a result of his outbursts, his marriage was in difficulty. His wife had also seen me and was clearly concerned about the future of their relationship and had even considered leaving him. His three teenage daughters were picking up the tension at home and starting to act out as a result, with the middle child becoming particularly rebellious.

Later, as I thought about the couple and their strained marriage, I had one of those "Ah Ha" moments. It became clear to me that in many ways this couple were actually mirror opposites. When I mentally listed their physical and emotional issues, there were a number of interesting contrasts:

• He had high blood pressure	She had low blood pressure.
• As much as he was active	She was passive (even lazy)
• He expressed his anger	She withdrew into silence
• He was extremely controlling	She was easily manipulated.
• He was self-centred (according to her)	She was overly concerned about everyone else's needs to the exclusion of her own.
• He was prone to emotional outbursts	She was cold emotionally
• He loved the sedative effects of marijuana	She enjoyed the stimulation of alcohol.
• He was large and powerfully built	She was frail and slim.
• He was domineering and controlling	She was fearful and withdrawn in the relationship

I sat there and thought that this could not just be co-incidence. I reviewed a second client:

• He suffered from serious *water* retention	She was arthritic (fire)
• He did not work	She never stopped
• He never went out	She went out the whole time
• He was passive aggressive	She expressed her anger
• He was completely non communicative	Her job was in communication
• He had no confidence	She was extremely confident
• He was seriously overweight	She was as thin as a rake
• He was the withdrawn child	She was the critical parent

I went to rummage through my clients' files and their histories and soon came to the realisation that each couple I was seeing or had seen, gay or straight, contained the polar opposites of the same issues. I was astounded that I had not come to what was now such an obvious revelation, sooner. I know the old saying opposites attract, but had never realised how deeply true this is, both physically and emotionally. I saw that each persons' relationship was either a polar opposite or that they were similar or a combination of both opposites and commonalities. Sometimes these would switch, depending on the situation or environments. However, the friction had arisen in the area of polar opposites. The reason they had been attracted to each other then, had become the reason they were having the most difficulties.

The concept made perfect sense. The universe is all about balance. As individuals this can be physically, such as finding a balance between alkalinity and excessive acidity or emotionally between being too angry and domineering or being so spineless that we allow others to trample all over us. As I examined the client notes that I make after each session, I realised why each couple had formed the relationship they had. In all their imperfection, they were the perfect match, in so far as they were perfectly suited for being the best potential for each others growth. For what better way to bring ourselves into balance than with the polar opposite of who we are. Where there are opposites, the potential for friction exists.

However, these people had come to me because they were unhappy within themselves, which was then projected onto their partners, who more often than not were identified as being the problem. Through understanding relationships as balance seeking mechanisms, all our partners' issues then become opportunities to identify our own potential for growth and transformation. Once we become aware of this see-saw effect, and change occurs within ourselves, then the dynamics of the relationship change and inevitably so does our partner.

The effect that one's personal transformation has on the relationships around us is an incredible experience to witness, where the seemingly impossible becomes possible. When we change and bring ourselves into balance, the outer world changes as a result. It has to be this way, because the entire universe is interconnected and nothing can change without it affecting everything else.

In this book we look at balancing the archetypal* and emotional seesaw within ourselves, so that we attract relationships that are in balance. I have used examples of couples to illustrate the kind of relationships that result when we are out of balance in certain areas, and how this affects a relationship. While you may not be able to identify exactly with each couple, elements of their relationship and its difficulties may help you understand the dynamics of your own relationship. Often simply understanding what is going on is sufficient to release that energy dynamic in the relationship. Relationships create games which require two people to play. (Try playing tennis or squash on a court on your own – it simply doesn't work). If one of you stops playing then the game must end.

This book then is aimed at helping you to understand what archetypal* roles are being played in your relationships, why they are being played, the cost to your happiness of continuing to do so and how to stop playing.

---

*(For the definition of archetypes see Chapter 4.)

Further, the whole book is essentially about balance. About reaching a point between the two polarised aspects of ourselves, represented by the hidden aspect (in our Shadow side) and the visible aspects which both swing out of control making us unbalanced and consequently not at peace with ourselves and our relationships. To heal ourselves and our relationships involves bringing ourselves into balance.

Note: For case histories, I have drawn from my experiences with people I have worked with and who have crossed my path in any number of ways. For their experiences as examples in this book, I am humbly grateful. In order to protect their identities however, I have changed all details that may identify them, keeping only the issues, as a way to demonstrate and assist others who may be able to identify with their experiences. Because we are working with archetypes of behaviour which are common to many, many of these cases overlay each other. So a number of people I have seen may in effect, all be represented by one case story told. As such, any resemblance to an actual person(s) is merely coincidental.

Chapter One

Why does Romeo become Rancid and Juliet become Jaded?

"Everything is Dual; everything has poles; everything has its pair of opposites; like and unlike are the same; opposites are identical in nature, but different in degree; extremes meet; all truths are but half-truths; all paradoxes may be reconciled.[1]"

–The Kybalion.

Your eyes meet across the room.

You feel him watching you, even though whenever you look in his direction, he appears to be engaged in conversation.

Eye connection occurs fleetingly and you both look quickly away, yet you are both intensely aware of each others presence, even though the room is impossibly crowded. He jostles towards you. Perhaps by chance? Then he makes a point of breaking into the group you are in. You feel relieved that it wasn't just you. Could this feeling be mutual? There is an attraction, something that says "Wow! Maybe coming to this party wasn't such a bad idea after all." He offers to get you a drink. You are terrified in case he doesn't come back. But he does. You do the small talk, find common interests, get ridiculously jealous when another woman embraces him, laugh at each others jokes, secretly imagine what he would be like without his clothes on and so the relationship continues. You agree to go out on a date; then a second - just to see where the relationship might lead. Besides, there are plenty of fish in the sea, but they are of little use unless you throw in a good line.

There's the excitement when you see him: the games, the touch, the tingle, the insecurities masked well with wine, the long calls, the crazy stuff like dancing without music, slurping the same piece of spaghetti, calling at 4am, intrigue perhaps in the form of ex lovers, parents, colleagues, frequent SMS's, telling your mates, wondering if your family will approve, then not caring whether they do, the initial awkwardness of the first time you make love... and from there, for some, a committed relationship.

At some stage though, the honeymoon is over.

It can take weeks, months or years and the relationship starts to show signs of wear and tear. Cracks appear in trust. Communication breaks down or is reduced to data downloading; withdrawn silences or angry outbursts become more frequent, and the make up time in between shorter and less intimate. Fears and accusations start to emerge and seem justified, extra stresses of finance, fidelity and addictions start to play a major role. Cleanliness issues, household chores, jealousy, unrealistic expectation of the other, start appearing. Sex becomes a tool of manipulation, used to make-up or is non-existent. Each person withdraws into a hole of bitter hurt and resentment between periods when it may seem all is well. Verbal abuse takes the place of words that were once loving and kind. Physical abuse turns the hero/ine that we loved into a horrific husband (or wife). Our world, once so full of promise, can seem like a harsh hell which we don't feel we deserve.

This situation can continue for months, years, or in many cases, a lifetime.

What happens to a relationship that takes all that was good and in such a short time make so much of it appear bad? Why does the sweetness of the honeymoon phase leave such a sour taste as time passes? Why does the person we once loved become the person we dislike the most?

In observing relationships, I have seldom seen one that truly is a relationship of choice where two people are together not simply because:

- they said a vow,
- they started going out and were never able to end it from there for fear of hurting the other
- it's the most economical way to live
- it's a habit they fear to break
- they fear change
- well doesn't everyone have problems?
- of the children
- religious beliefs
- they are enmeshed because of a job situation, financial issue etc
- what others would say if they separated (families, religious groups etc)
- it's better than being alone
- financial security
- it's not THAT bad
- or there doesn't appear to be another viable option,

But because they have a deep and genuine desire to assist their partners to grow spiritually, as well as truly feeling inspired and uplifted in each others presence.

How many of us can honestly say our relationships fall into the later category? Why is this so? Why does Romeo become rancid and Juliet become jaded?

Why the puzzle no longer fits

What happens initially in the "honeymoon" phase of a relationship, is that we believe we have found the missing piece of our inner personal relationship puzzle – the person who makes us feel whole. Up to now we felt like a piece of ourselves was missing. We are elated with the fit initially. Everything seems so perfect. We have found our soulmate surely?

In not being whole or complete ourselves (and very, very few people are), we seek someone to make us feel whole or complete and we project onto them, all that we would like to be. If we are shy, we seek someone who is outgoing and who appears confident. If we are emotionally withdrawn, we desire someone who is warm and who can openly express their emotions. If we are a driven A-type personality, someone who is laid-back could spark our romantic flame.

In time, as we grow and change, the pieces of the puzzle don't fit as comfortably and lovingly as they used to. Naturally, we blame the other person for changing or not, as the case may be. Where is the person who I could not wait to see? Whose touch drove me wild with desire? Whose emails did I sit around for hours waiting for? Whose opinion did I value above all else? What in fact went wrong with Mr. Right? Now we feel as if the two pieces don't fit, yet alone we don't feel whole either.

The cruel illusion is that we projected what we wanted onto another person, as they did with us. The realisation comes the day when we discover they are not the person we believed them to be. We are angry with them for not being the person we believe we desire – the unresolved aspects of ourselves. We have placed expectations on them that are unreal. Why should they be the way we want them to be anymore than why should we live up to their expectations? The puzzle is falling to pieces and they are no longer a perfect fit for us.

When the honeymoon is over, somebody has to make the bed.
And then there were two – the nature of duality

The entire universe is based on duality. As such it is a balance seeking mechanism.

Right wrong. Day night. Good evil. Matter anti-matter. Sun moon. Water fire. Contraction expansion. Acid alkaline. Positive charge negative charge. Anode cathode. Wet dry. Male female. Ego and the higher self. Positive negative. Creation destruction. Passive active. Individual collective. Cold hot. Intuition logic. Subtraction addition. Yin yang. War peace. Matter spirit. White holes black holes. Exhalation inhalation. Balance imbalance. Left and right, are only a few of the many examples in our universe.

This push/pull between opposites is the driving force in the universe.

It affects all things in creation, from the largest galaxy to the smallest atom including our lives. All things are subject to this duality. If we follow biblical and many other ancient teachings, we can see we originated from one – Adam, and became two when Eve was formed. The desire not only in us as humans, but in the entire universe is to seek wholeness or put another way, to reach balance. Relationships are our external attempt to reach this state. (In truth this state has to be reached internally before it can manifest externally).

All physical, emotional and mental dysfunction has its origin in imbalance.

Even as God from his One created a polar opposite in Lucifer, so we create our own world of polar opposites and then strive again to become One. Relationships are all about finding our opposites in another, in an attempt to balance ourselves.

Into me see.

If we listen to the sound of the word "intimacy," it can be broken down into three words: *into me see,* in other words to have intimacy requires that we see into the other person's soul. It means being completely non judgemental and having unconditional acceptance of someone. Believing that your partner should be x, y, or z before this can be achieved, is a contradiction, because what you are really saying is I'll love you on my conditions, (which as we know is not really love). Love by its nature is unconditional. You can't love someone and want them to be any other way, than that which they are. Instead of seeing what they are, you see rather what they are not and in focusing on this lack of whatever, you miss seeing the true wondrousness of their being.

Why do we all crave intimacy? And we all do, no matter what our age, sex, or belief system; we long for this complete acceptance and will devote huge amounts of time and effort in pursuit of this often elusive goal. At times, during the start of a relationship we may feel we have found this – just watch lovers in a crowd together, they are completely absorbed in each other and what in later years they may find offensive about each other, is at this stage, yet another reason to desire the other.

At the same time if we don't accept ourselves completely, we're not in a position to do the same for another. If intimacy is about complete acceptance and relationships are mirrors for ourselves, then in accepting someone else, we also accept ourselves completely and vice versa.

How does this feel? A friend explained it to me like this: "He was a client of mine, however I could not help notice that he was tall, drop dead gorgeous with the sort of body that only comes with being a superb athlete. My mind kept on wanting to go to the possibility of a romance even though practically, the situation was far from ideal. My thinking and fantasizing had got me completely."

"Already I had expectations and was losing energy to them. (Because with an expectation comes the fear of a goal not being successful, and fear drains our energy). "Rather than go there, (in terms of jumping into bed with him), I asked myself what he was mirroring to me about myself. Suddenly I saw in him aspects of myself: I felt waves of compassion for him and myself. I reached a point, through self observation and through dropping my thinking and reaching a state of being, where I no longer identified with my expectations towards him, meaning I was detached from my expectations."

"I saw his struggles, his insecurities, his courage, his need for intimacy etc. In seeing the wholeness of him, a strange thing occurred. It was as if there was intense light around him. I thought it was just me, but he said he observed the same light around myself. For minutes we did not speak, but rather just sat there, bathed in light and complete acceptance. There was such love between us. It was as if there was no separation. Yet there was no romantic/sexual aspect at all. After the experience the need for a relationship as such with him was gone and filled with a deeper awe at what happens when we connect with someone or something else at a really deep level. We did become one."

This becoming one, is what true intimacy is about. We want to become one with all that is and most of all Divinity; this is the ultimate – to experience union or oneness with God (or whatever our concept of that being is) and all that is. When we experienced the Fall as written about in the Bible, we believed we were cast out or separated from this oneness. Relationships, provide us with a means of obtaining this goal – a step on the rung to achieving wholeness or holiness.

Relationships give us enormous potential to grow as human beings. They are where we have the opportunity to grow the most, but they are also where most people endure great suffering.

Through many years of observing relationships, I have come to understand that they are an attempt to bring ourselves into balance. We sit on one side of the see-saw and are attracted to someone who will balance the see-saw for us. However, soon what attracts us, also repels us. Because whatever we find irritating about another person inevitably ends up being some aspect of our own imbalance, either as it is or in its opposite form. Rather than own this in ourselves, we resent it in another.

The person who dislikes the fact that their partner is scattered, overly inflexible and never seems to complete anything, will discover that they themselves carry the same or opposite trait: namely rigidity or inflexibility, the inability to move from a set course of action, even when it is clear that it no longer serves them and the focus on one thing, to the exclusion of all else. The game we play then is to blame the other person for their "faults," as a means of avoiding facing the more uncomfortable idea that we are part of the imbalance.

I have come to see that the deficient and excessive aspects of problematic issues are mirrored in most peoples' relationships. By understanding what we dislike in our partner, we have a profound clue as to where we are not in balance, for both our wounds inevitably then are similar. That's why we come together with someone - to heal our wound which is reflected in them.

What we perceive as our perfect match, is the balance we need to feel whole.

In other words we choose our partners (and their wounds) in an attempt to find the matching piece of our own wounded psychological jigsaw. We look for the perfect match, not realising that because we are wounded in certain ways (and very few of us are not) on a deep unconscious level we pair up with the mirror image of our own wound, in the guise of our partner, in an attempt to become whole.

However, no other person can make us feel whole. Only within ourselves can we be this, so inevitably the relationship where two halves are attempting to make a whole, must fail, or at best be fraught with discontent. It is only when two people, both of whom feel whole or complete within themselves pair up, that the relationship can truly be one of dynamic growth. The word "*part*ner" itself suggests that each person is only a "part" and needs another then to be whole.

Instead of simply viewing the psychology of relationships themselves we can:

- analyse why the sexes are different,
- focus on past events,
- seek to analyze why the other person may be a certain way,
- understand relationships and balance,
- bring ourselves into the present time, to understand that all we have to do for situations to change, is to change ourselves and the relationship inevitably will change.

Imagine you were sitting on a see-saw with your partner at the opposite end. You cannot alter your position on a see-saw without it affecting the person on the other side. It goes against the laws of the universe. Your moving up or down on the see-saw will affect the person sitting on the other end. The closer you get to the centre, the less the see-saw swings from side to side i.e. the less you have extreme conflicts etc and the more you get together in the place of centeredness, in other words create true balance which allows for intimacy in your relationship.

This is not an easy concept to acknowledge, (pointing fingers is much more appealing!) However, if we truly want more fulfilling relationships where we can grow into more enlightened human beings, there can be few better places to start, than examining our relationships and their imbalances.

Intimacy and sex

Tinker, tailor, soldier, sailor, model and nun, we all crave intimacy, once we have our basic needs of food and shelter.

Some seek it in its highest form i.e. with the Divine/God, but most of us seek it from our fellow man (or woman). It's what drives us into relationships and the lack of it breaks our heart and sets us on a renewed path to find its elusive manna.

Along the way, we get confused and may, especially if we are a man, believe that what we are craving is sex, when in reality we are seeking something infinitely more. That's not to say that every time we want sex it's because we want intimacy, but we can mix our desire for sex with a desire for intimacy. Intimacy does not necessarily equal sex. It may form a part of it, but it is very possible to be intimate and not sexual, as the previous story showed. In fact, the work of most sexual therapists is to teach couples intimacy as a path to more fulfilling sex. Whereas we tend to have sex in the hope that intimacy will result. When it doesn't, we may feel empty and blame our partner, or rush off to find another partner, in the hope that they'll fill the gap in our lives.

Commonly men seek sex in order to have intimacy, while women seek intimacy in order to have sex.

If you are the type of person who craves sex with every Tom, Dick and Harry, (or Mum, Britt and Carrie), you could look at what it is you are really looking for. Is it only a physical craving? Is it a desire to woo and conquer? Or is there a deeper need you can't ever seem to fulfil?

In seeking intimacy what we seek is wholeness or hol(y)ness. We feel incomplete and deep within our subconscious, lies the desire to become whole or One with all that is. This desire triggers our need to have relationships, hoping that by doing so we will find in our partner the lost pieces of ourselves. When we fall in love we see the "other" as fulfilling this role. We become one or whole, only to drift apart later when our partner no longer seems to complete us.

When there is imbalance or anger/hurt in a relationship, sex is often the first thing to decrease or disappear all together. When a man is not feeling a man (often through losing a job, feeling he can't contribute enough to the income, or being made to feel inadequate by his partner), he will show his feelings of inadequacy through not feeling worthy of sex with his partner. In nature the stronger more confident males get to mate more, in humans it's much the same. When a woman is feeling frustrated or resentful towards her partner, sex is usually the tool she withdraws to make her (often silent) resentment felt.

In saying why they have little desire for sex with their partner, (as opposed to a lack of sexual desire in general), women will commonly name three things as being the reason:

- lack of hygiene,
- lack of technique
- and lack of help in the home

Lack of Hygiene

Smell plays a more important role in sex than most people realise. Although we are not conscious of it, both sexes respond to the smell of each other and men can detect when a woman is ovulating simply by an increase in desire for her. (*The Journal of Evolution and Human Behaviour* published a study showing that strippers who are ovulating make double the tips as opposed to those who are menstruating.)[1]

If your partner smells unpleasantly, to your subconscious filtering system which determines who will or won't make a good mate, a bad smell is equivalent to, for example, rotting meat, which in nature is likely to mean that a person may carry a disease. It's natural then that we will withdraw from this encounter and look for something with better prospects for us and our survival.

Lack of technique

Most men expect that they should know how a woman's body functions. It's somehow not acceptable to admit to your jock buddies that you don't know how to pleasure a woman. This perception is fast shifting and more men are accepting the responsibility for their own sexual performance realising that a better and more satisfying act mutually, is also more pleasing to them and ensures more frequency of sex.

However, there are still those men who either through ignorance or arrogance, think sex is about reaching orgasm the fastest way possible. If you can relate to this with regard to your partner, then maybe it;s time to examine your own sexuality, so that you can gently and with encouragement, rather than criticism, demonstrate to your partner what works for you. (Most men are keen pupils when it comes to sex)!

Help in the home

It's hard for some men (and also some women in same sex relationships) to understand that cleaning the dishes or changing a nappy, is a precursor to a successful

---

[1] http://www.time.com/time/magazine/article/0,9171,1704672-2,00.html The Science of Romance: Why We Love. Thursday, Jan. 17, 2008. By JEFFREY KLUGER

sexual experience, but in most relationships it is. (Which could just be the reason for the word women sounding like "Woe Men!")

Many men (and some women) have been brought up to believe that they are somehow above helping. They may have had mothers or servants who did it all for them. In many countries with a colonial background, children of the wealthier classes, get used to having everything done for them by a host of servants. When in a relationship the same expectation can continue, so that it doesn't even occur to the person to help which can be very frustrating to their hard working partner. The classic idea of a subservient wife has not helped the situation. Then the ideal woman was one who was seen to cater for her husband's every need, (her needs were not important.) Some men have carried this concept into the new millennium.

Getting back to nature, a female will only mate if she has a good nest, there is a good supply of food and other such basic requirements are fulfilled. Humans are much the same when it comes to choosing a mate. If you are feeling resentful and angry (as well as exhausted) after cooking, caring, working and cleaning unaided, you will in all likelihood withhold sex. Your withdrawing, will mean your partner will also withdraw to the other end of the see-saw or will express his/her anger. If you could communicate and thus move closer to balancing the situation, for the sake of yet another game on TV, you could have wild, wondrous sex.

Other reasons we don't have sex

It's estimated that around 40 million Americans have marriages where they don't have sex. I have been surprised to find out just how many relationships are celibate or pretty close to celibate. Some reasons are:

- Medication. With 40 million people on antidepressants some of which are believed to reduce sexual drive, it's not surprising that many people are experiencing a loss of libido. But it's not only anti-depressant medications which can affect sexual drive; many other medications can have a similar reaction. Depression itself reduces the sex drive.
- Too much external stimulation. The average 1950's woman was more sexually active than her modern day counterpart. With the busyness of our lives, coupled with TV's in the bedroom and other gadgets such as computers, sms- ing its not hard to understand why that may be so
- Too much pressure on performing. Practically every glossy magazine carries at least one article telling us how to make love perfectly. Whereas in the past it was a more take it or leave it affair, men are under huge pressure, particu-

larly with a new partner, to perform at peak. Sometimes then, rather than face failure it's easier just to opt out.

- Communication has broken down in the relationship to the extent that sex is a non event.

- Severe emotional turmoil. If you've been let down badly you may associate this with sex, so that every time sex is imminent it sparks off a subconscious fear of the rejection you have experienced and you respond by...well not responding.

- Another problem created by the media is that of the "perfect body." We believe it exists (just not on us,) so we feel ashamed of our bumps and lumps and become unwilling to reveal them to another. Even models and movie stars can suffer from this "I hate my body syndrome," to the detriment of their sex life.

- Peri-menopause and menopause. As our hormones fluctuate we can often experience a loss of libido. As they say, "of *men a pause*!"

- Boredom. Same old, same old. Sometimes when you've been with a partner for a long time, sex can lose its sizzle.

- Illness. Simply not feeling up to it. Many illnesses can leave us feeling tired or in pain, in which case sex is the last thing we want.

- Masturbation is easier, less pressurised and comes with less emotional baggage than having to risk rejection or criticism from a partner.

Chapter Two

What builds and what breaks relationships

I'm OK, you're not OK – Judgement and the need to be right.

If I'm right you must be wrong.

"If only he/she would change...." "He/she has changed so much since we first became involved," how many times do we say something similar about our partner?

You see we seem to have a fundamental belief that goes something along the lines of: "if my partner would only change his/her behaviour, then my life will be great, but until that happens, I am forced to suffer in a relationship that is not making me happy and which I can't do anything about."

Having now put the onus of our happiness firmly onto the shoulders of our partners' errant ways, we can now sit back expectantly and wait for the miracle to happen. When it doesn't, (which it seldom, if ever does), we feel we have just cause to live in quiet (and sometimes not so quiet) resentment. In doing so we live, as Descartes the French Philosopher said, "Lives of quiet desperation."

There are many aspects to each relationship and many ways for each person involved to tell their "truth". The problem comes when each party believes their truth to be THE truth which equates to one persons' "truth" being right, (in which case the other's must be wrong). Most of the time we all believe we are right, which equates to two rights in a relationship which naturally then creates two version of what is wrong. This model of relationship is destined at worst to fail and at very best to see-saw between periods of okayness and between lives of resentment and frustration. (And we enter into relationships believing they will make us happier people!)

Two women came knocking at my door. They wanted to convert me to their belief system. I was told that their faith (and in particular their particular branch of their faith), was the only way to God. All other paths were wrong. I did appreciate the time and effort these women put into what they felt was my hope for salvation and treated them cordially. However, I had to point out that a few days before, someone else had knocked on my door with the same reasoning, only they were from a different church.

I asked the people with whom I was now having a conversation, the question as to which of them were right. From a neutral position, it was only logical to see that if both their paths were the only path, then for one to be right, the other must be wrong. In which case I asked, which of them spoke the truth and which was lying? According to both there was only one truth – theirs and the rest was the untruth or the enemy. It's not difficult to see that a world filled with this mind set, is a world that is filled with paranoia and conflict. Everyone who does not think and believe as I do then, is the enemy which must be destroyed, which pretty much describes the world we live in.

Why has this mindset occurred? Precisely because of the need to be right. If I need to be right and so do you, then there will inevitably be conflict as I attempt to dominate you with my right(eous)ness. Of course the world cannot always agree with our version of right which will leave us constantly frustrated and unhappy. Why can't everyone else, think, act, have the same beliefs, have the same morals, values, good habits and generally just be like me? In expecting our relationships to be this way we are constantly going to be disappointed. Why does the difference in others cause us so much pain?

Simply because we fear deep down that their way may be better than ours. We are tribal beings and anyone who is not like us, is then from a different tribe. What has happened in history between rival tribes? Yes, that's right – lots of fighting/wars. So when someone is not like us, it creates separateness which creates fear, which we often express through conflict. (This has biblical connotations in the separation and the inevitable Fall, because deep down any separateness reminds us of the illusion that we are separate from God/the Divine).

Difference = Separateness = Fear

In having a different belief system or way of being from ours, our ego, which by its nature, embodies inadequacy, sees their difference as being a potential threat to us and responds in anger/fear to protect itself. It comes from a belief in separateness as opposed to oneness. The more different we feel, the more separated or isolated we perceive ourselves to be. This feeling different or isolated, inevitably is translated into our psyche as feeling better or worse than someone else. Which translates into our interactions as being arrogant or as is more often the case, into feeling inadequate (the mirror of arrogance), which is where our ego loves us to be. Why? Because to the extent that we feel inadequate, is to the extent that the ego is in charge. Separation, divisions in beliefs, families, organisations and relationships feeds the ego at the expense of our authentic selves. It's the old concept of divide and rule. The more you move away from being whole (holy) or integrated, the more scattered or fragmented you feel and the more your ego will rule your roost and the lower your self-esteem will be.

As long as we hold the concept of we/they, we create much pain and suffering in ours and the lives of others. We also reduce our own potential for joy because if things aren't "right," we can't be happy. So much effort going into proving we are right, or wanting things to be right, comes at the expense of simply enjoying the moment.

Beating the opposition – Competition in relationships

Competition is common in relationships, especially when two fiery people are involved. Fire likes to win, but to win means having to have someone to compete against. Naturally you could look for that someone at the office or in your bed. Even if they are not particularly interested in competing with you, your desire to win will see you looking for a challenge in some way. What happens then when the less competitive partner ends up "winning?"

It will naturally cause the other partner to slip to the end of the see-saw into the space marked "loser." This is not a good feeling, so it's natural that to avoid this in future, we may consciously or sub-consciously attempt to sabotage the other person's success. Not essentially because we don't want them to win (although this can happen) but more because we don't want to feel a failure in comparison.

These Winner and Loser titles can create havoc in a relationship. Winning means to be right about everything, in order for one person then to "win," the other person has to "lose." If you are not able to hold onto your rightness (being righteous) then the huge fear you carry is that you are wrong i.e. a failure. When people have to be right about everything, know then that the reason they will continue to fight even when proven wrong, is because conceding is yet another indication of their failure. (More of the Success and Failure, archetypes follows later in Chapter 14.

It reminds me of the photograph of a huge traffic circle in Italy with all the cars, bar one, going in the same direction. The owner of the car going the opposite way is hanging out of his car yelling at all the other motorists for going the wrong way.

Jason was a person whose need to be right made him socially less enjoyable to be with. When he put forward his view, he was right. No question about it. Woe betides anyone who questioned it. Scream, throw a tantrum, hurt those he loved, be verbally abusive – he resorted to any and all of these tactics in order to maintain his rightness. Even when he was shown to be irrefutably incorrect on some matter, rather than accept the proof, he would fly off in another direction of argument about an unrelated matter, where he could endorse his view that he and only he was right (and everyone else had got it wrong).

As he aged, and became more insecure so his need to be right increased, destroying relationships and making him desperately unhappy. However, the pay off of being right (as an attempt to boost himself), was worth the unhappy drama and alienation it created. This need to win at all costs and be right can be extremely debilitating in a relationship, because it creates a "we/they" thinking. (This is another way of saying that it constantly reinforces your position at the opposite end of the see-saw where intimacy is not possible.)

It also affects our ability to listen. We are so busy being right that we will not listen to our partner's point of view – there's no point, ours is right after all. This makes for very difficult communication in a relationship, as the other person does not feel heard, and as a result feels frustrated and resentful.

A simple method to work with this issue, if you recognise it in your relationship is to create the discipline of reflecting back to your partner what it is they have said, irrespective as to whether you agree or not. Just letting your partner know that you have understood their view without judging it can be hugely therapeutic in creating meaningful communication. Much of the work at Lifeline where I was a volunteer, involved just reflecting back to the caller what they had said, rather than attempting to work the problem out for them.

Commonly when confronted with a friend or partner with a problem, most men will want to solve the problem, where women are more inclined to listen but not feel the need to find a solution.

If your partner were to say: "I'm fed up with this house looking like a bomb's exploded in it, why can't it look neat for once." This is a potential hand grenade. You could respond by saying: "you ungrateful bastard, I have washed, cleaned and cooked the whole damn day, but you try to maintain a tidy house with two kids. If it worries you so much you sort it out." Bang. Now the hand grenade's really exploded!

Or you could use the reflecting exercise: "I understand that it is frustrating for you to come back after a difficult day at the office and find things not right at home."

"Yes," he may continue, "it's been a really bad day, I think we may have messed up a large order and Jim is holding me directly responsible."

You could further reflect, "I can see that would be a most uncomfortable position to be in and it can't feel good having your capabilities questioned."

What you are doing here is calming him down, showing that you understand him and realising that the attack initially was more about his fear of losing his job than the state of the house. Now he is ready to share with you his anxieties as opposed to entering into conflict.

If the man in this scenario were to adopt a similar approach of reflecting your feelings back to you, both of you would feel far more intimate and close to each other and you would meet at the centre point of the see-saw.

Somewhere between the desire to win or be right and the fear of failing, lies acceptance and understanding.

I travelled to a remote place in Fiji, where I met a man who had been a cannibal. We were on an idyllic island, where there were fish aplenty, a hot water spring, many yams, coconuts, paw-paws and bananas, as well as the narcotic kava-kava root, which the local people use as a relaxant (looks like mud when it's drunk and has a numbing effect on the tongue). Everything seemed so blissful it was hard to believe that tribes on the island and on similar neighbouring islands could find any reason whatsoever to wage war. Yet they used to, with the ferocity that saw them chomping away on their defeated enemies. One can only conclude they fought simply because they saw each tribe as different to them and therefore a threat. (There were also the obvious advantages of raping and pillaging which would have strengthened each tribe and helped to overcome inbreeding).

Accepting ownership of what is happening in our life is a huge step to regaining the power we have lost along the way. However accepting responsibility is hard and consequently, this book may not be a comfortable book to read – it's so more therapeutic to believe that it is the other person who is out of line and needs to change, rather than accept that responsibility ourselves. Assuming responsibility for our lives, and that includes our relationships, is not a particularly attractive concept to most of us. Making our partner wrong so we can be right, is a far easier groove to slip into and yet while we do so we remain chained to unfulfilling co-dependant relationships lacking in true intimacy.

A brief look at the ego

What actually is the ego? Is it really bad? Should we have one or should we be trying not to?

Much gets written about the ego, often making it a confusing subject. In my understanding, the ego was a term coined by Sigmund Freud, (together with Id and super-ego) to define the human psyche. The word ego comes from Latin and can be translated as "I myself," or "the I." He associated it with denial, displacement, projection, repression, regression, compensation and intellectualisation.

However, since then the term has come to describe our lower selves.

The archetypes we will examine later in the book are a projection of our ego. Transcending them is to transcend the ego based self. Whereas our higher self is about seeing the Divine in everything including ourselves, the ego will thrive on belittling the self. It is the part of us that encourages one to break disciplines and then it is the same part that will criticise us for our weaknesses. The more you live in the negative emotions of pain, guilt, jealousy, shame etc the more the ego thrives. It is the foe, (described in mythology and fairytales as the Dragon, the witch or the ogre) that needs to be destroyed if you are to become whole or enlightened. It is what makes us arrogant, when we are really insecure, assume our own righteousness, while making others wrong, it thrives on approval seeking and dominating and manipulating others. Separation and alienation are its friend, oneness the enemy.

In creating these divisions, the ego creates the big illusion that we are separate. A sort of "we – they" thinking. The ego will seek to punish you and scorn you for your "wrong-doing," while your higher self will forgive you, show compassion for you and support your efforts in trying to become more whole.

To experience duality we need to experience the illusion of separation from our higher selves and the Divine. In overcoming the ego, we come to the realisation that all is one and we see the Divine spark in everything and everyone.

Expectation in relationships

A big reason many relationships fail, is due to false expectations.

Here you are sitting on your end of the see-saw, waiting for someone to come along to balance things out. Now you have certain ideas of what you are looking for and when someone comes along and the chemistry starts working, the expectations that you have had get imposed on this person. Whoopee! Equilibrium on the see-saw.

However it is a very uneasy equilibrium as it's based on our expectations, rather than reality.

Expectations cause imbalance.

The more we project through our expectations out "there" the less "here" we are. Buddhist philosophy, as one of their key teachings, encourages the disciple to let go of expectations. Why should anyone respond to your way of being? The more you expect your partner to be a certain way, the more you set your see-saw up for a bumpy up and down relationship. The more you release the need for anyone or anything to be a certain way, the more you free yourself up from stress and conflict.

Expectation is the opposite of acceptance.

This is a hard principle to work with. I mean if the light bulb needs changing or the dishwasher needs unloading, and you feel you've done your bit, not expecting the other person to do anything seems downright unfair. Yet see what happens. You expect. They resist, (if there is already tension). You get resentful and angry. Whoosh, off you slide down the see-saw, while they withdraw to the other end. So the expectation has only caused suffering for you. (They are unaware of your expectation and are unaffected). Whenever there is an expectation, be it to win the lotto, to want your child to follow a certain career path, or expect a person to behave the way you want them to, you set yourself up for disappointment.

In our minds, expectations achieved = success. Expectations not achieved = failure.

Many times in my life things have not worked out the way I had expected them to and in hindsight, what happened was perfect, even though at the time I may have felt this was not the case. (And sometimes what seemed perfect turned out not to be so.)

Not having expectations, does not mean we should not have goals, just that we should not attach our energy to their outcome. It's really a case of trusting the universe to give to us exactly what we need, when we need it, in order to grow.

Needing approval

Whenever we need approval we create the opposite potential of having somebody disprove of us.

You see, when I wait for you to approve of me, what I am really doing is handing over my power to you. If you want to control me, (and most of us rather enjoy controlling others), then all I have to do to remain in control of you, is withdraw the approval you are looking for.

The result?

You'll keep trying harder to win my approval. Don't you know of situations where one child will do everything to try to please (get approval from) the parents, while another child in the same family will not give a care for parental approval. Most often the parents will idolise this child. Paradoxically the more we seek others approval, the less we get it and the more we reject this need, the more we are approved and liked.

This need for approval is deep-rooted in each and everyone of us. To the extent that our self esteem is diminished, is to the extent we will seek it. The harder we try to win the approval of others, the more we will suppress our own needs and desires, to do so. This craving for approval then costs us the ability to express our authentic selves. We are so busy being what we feel others want us to be, that we forget who we are. This creates a feeling of: "I will only be loved if I behave/do/act in a certain way." The harder we try to be what we are not, for the sake of winning the approval of others, the further we get from who we really are.

This creates resentment and frustration. A feeling of "I am being loved for what I do not for who I am." Or "no-one really understands or sees the real me." This bending to the desires of others, comes at the cost of our own self-expression. We feel we can't be or express who we truly are (no one may like us then). This in itself creates an imbalance between the authentic me, and the projected me, played out in various archetypal roles.

Rule the Fool

Dominating is another way we act in relationships and is an indication that we are not in balance. When we need to control those around us we create a need for our partners to withdraw or rebel. (More of this can be seen in the Tyrant/Victim/Rebel archetypes dealt with later in the book). This need to be in charge can take up a huge amount of energy, as we run around controlling our minions. The result is that the ruler often finds themselves exhausted from "doing everything" yet won't allow others to do anything for fear of losing control.

Chapter Three

Fire and Rain

Opposite elements and their relation to us

To examine the issues involved in relationships, we need to look at the elemental principles of male and females energies within each of us.

Fire is the male element, while the female element is water. Balance between the two elements represented as male and female energy is crucial to a balanced and thriving relationship. These polar opposites, comprise the essence of male energy and female energy, irrespective of what bodies they happen to be in. By this I mean that a man may be very watery (female energy) and a woman more fiery (male energy). Both energies are present in each of us; it's the amount that varies.

This subtle balance is not visible in humans alone. If we step back and look at the planet, these forces are constantly at play. Too much heat/fire and you have a drought. Too much water and you have floods. A balance between sufficient rain and heat from the sun, creates the best environment for the planet to thrive. Another way to look at it, is through the balance between sea and land. As the polar ice caps melt, they create more sea/water which looks to upset the fragile balance in the world and could result in cataclysmic floods, tidal waves and natural disasters.

The same can be said to be true of ourselves. Too much water and we are overly emotional and introverted. Too much fire, and we are quick to anger and can be so busy doing, we can burn out.

Let's go back to the principles of fire and water.

Fire

The element of fire as mentioned is associated with masculine energy. It has the power to destroy and transform. It is outgoing, as it gives out heat and is an active principal (as opposed to passive). In our language we speak of a *hot-blooded* young man, meaning that he is full of passion and often anger, attributes more commonly associated with male energy. We talk about, a guy we fancy as being "*hot.*" We get "*fired up,*" about a project. We "*set the world on fire,*" when we create a difference or make our presence known. Likewise, phrases such as having a "*fiery temperament,*" a *burning desire,* a *heated argument,* a *flaming row, my old flame* (as in the person who *set my heart on fire,*) are all associated with the element of fire. This fiery element is associated with the sun, daytime and going outwards to explore and experience.

Water

Water is associated with feminine energy.

It is less active and flows according to the shape of the earth, thus it is more passive. We speak of someone being a *drip,* feeling *washed out,* being a *wet* (no courage or fiery male energy) or being *watered down,* all as a description of having little energy or passion or being weakened. *Going with the flow* speaks of a lack of fiery resistance. While fire is hot, traditionally, water is cool. It's not so much that female energy is weak, just less active and more accepting or receptive. (Just think about our sex organs and the act of sex itself – the male organ is out there and penetrative, while the female is receptive and traditionally more passive in the act.) The feminine moon is associated with night and going inwards in order to learn. This act of going within is found in words that mirror this concept, such as in-tuition, introvert, insight, etc.

When fire and water combine

The perception has often been, that water/feminine energy is weak, but this is not so. When water and fire combine, water, has the ability to destroy a fire by smothering it, while conversely fire can evaporate water and thus eliminate it. At this level then, the two forces become destructive to each other. There is then, a subtle balance between water and fire. At its best, fiery heat balances the coolness of water, and water balances the dryness of fire, which creates the potential for growth. As an example, if a dry, hot, arid soil is rained upon, it becomes moist and creates an environment suitable for plants to thrive. This delicate balance of not too much rain, resulting in a flood and not too little, resulting in a drought, is what keeps an eco system surviving. Mess with this and the entire system collapses. Keep it in balance and it thrives.

We are no different. When out of balance we create destruction and havoc in our lives, when in balance, peace, joy, harmony and the ability to develop ourselves further as human beings, is the result.

When we are out of balance we take this inner turmoil and project it onto our relationships with others. The point is, the turmoil starts within and we project it into our world.

Our choice of partners is part of this projection. If we are for instance very fiery, (quick to anger,) a workaholic and enjoy dominating those around us, we will seek balance in the form of someone who is watery and has for instance a compliant or passive nature, who finds it hard to self-motivate. So we are drawn to other people's fire or water as a way to balance ourselves.

However, in seeking them as a form of balance, we will also find them a constant source of irritation simply because they are not like us. What initially attracted us to them now repels us and the irony is we lay the blame on them for not being more like us.

Examining relationships bearing these two aspects in mind, will help us to see where our own relationships are out of balance. By understanding the fire and water principle, we can balance ourselves in order to bring joy, harmony and opportunities to grow.

Water, the feminine energy, like the archetypal female flows or yields and is a passive element. Other water or female attributes would include:

- Nurturing
- Gentleness
- Moist or wetness
- Intuition
- Emotion/feeling/heart
- Surrendering/allowing
- Insightfulness
- Exhalation
- Left side
- Circular or flowing shapes
- Passivity
- Cold

Male or fire attributes are active and transformative and would include:

- Creating
- Harshness
- Dry or aridness
- Logic
- Thinking/head
- Controlling/organisation
- Asserting
- Expressive
- Inhalation
- Right side

- Rod or straight lines
- Active
- Heat

Each of us carry a combination of these elements and depending on which of these aspects is most dominant, we could be said to be either fiery or watery, no matter what sex we are.

The more these elements within us are out of balance, the more the relationships will see-saw between bliss and bedlam. For fiery passion to exist, requires watery surrender. If there is not this balance, the situation is too fiery, causing it to ignite and become explosive. If there is watery submissiveness from both people, the relationship will become cold, insular and boring, often with passive aggressive elements. This may take the form of everything appearing to be OK on the surface and yet beneath, runs a deep undercurrent of hostility, which constantly sabotages the relationship and any hope of true intimacy.

At the start of a relationship we may swing between fiery passion and watery emotions. We burn with passion, we feel energised, alive. We surrender to our passions and go with the flow of our loved ones desires. For a while we have the illusion of being one with each other. In time however, we start a gradual process of separation and the One becomes us and them. The aspects that represent what we fell in love with, in representing the polar opposites of ourselves, now become the aspects that we least like about the other person. Why? Because those aspects or their polar opposites reside within our selves often in our shadow selves, where we don't really want to acknowledge them.

We then draw on those same elements that bonded us, to break each other down. In that we move between wanting to change the other person (fire transforms) to surrendering to their demands or needs (water gives way). Caught between silently and resentfully complying and hostilely demanding or expectantly wanting our partner to change, we become stuck in a relationship that offers little in the way of happiness or intimacy.

You may fall in love with his ability to take command (fire). In time however that same ability appears more as a need to dominate and control you and naturally you resent being dominated. To balance this, you may withdraw and seek to manipulate/control him in other ways. Or his quiet artistic romantic ways may make him stand out from a crowd of jocks who bore you. Two years down the road and you resent his passivity (water) which you now see as being spineless. This mirrors your own fear of standing up for yourself. (Lack of fire.)

If male energy is threatened, the response is fire/anger.

If female energy is threatened it responds in water/tears.

As most men are predominately more fiery and women more watery it stands to reason that most women cry (water) when they are angry and most men get angry (fire) when they are afraid or sad.

Women are afraid often to express their fire and men their water. Because of the polarisation in society, men are often not comfortable with their own female side and many women believe that to act on their male side, is to be unfeminine – it's just not nice!

What happens when a man carries too much fire, is that he becomes over dominating and controlling. Dan was just such a man. He could not let his wife out of his sight without the need to call and check she was ok, often several times a night. This may appear to be a loving trait, but in truth his need for control did not allow her any peace when out of his sight. She felt claustrophobic in his presence. Being watery, she was unable to express her anger and so withdrew emotionally and sexually. This increased his fire making him more controlling and quick to anger when she did not answer her cellphone immediately. The situation spiralled downwards, as his fire increased so did her water, in the form of depression (depression = repressed aggression or fire withheld which we unconsciously try to balance by becoming watery or depressed).

With both males and females suppressing their opposite polar emotion, what is repressed gets expressed in a shadow way and externalised on our partner, who we then see as the enemy (which is inevitably lurking within our own psyche.)

What we dislike in others, is what we dislike most in ourselves.

Take the elderly spinster who disapproves most vehemently of flirtatious young women with questionable (by her standards) morals. What is happening here? She has never lived out her sensual/sexual aspect of herself which lurks in her shadow. Not being capable or wanting to acknowledge this within herself, she fears it in others which she expresses as disapproval. Yet a part of her longs and may even fantasize about this hidden unexplored aspect of herself, or it may appear in dreams where she is doing wild and wondrous sexual things with the vicar which on waking, she may understandably not want to remember, so her subconscious conveniently deletes the "naughty" bits. Yet still they remain in her shadow and are reflected in every sexy woman she meets, which is why she becomes angry.

Children and Fire and Water

In a relationship where both parents are more fiery, the chances are good that at least one of the children will be more watery to bring the family unit into balance. Not having much fire then, this watery child could bare the brunt of much of the parents' fiery anger, sometimes to the point of abuse. The parent(s) wants fire from the child and when only water appears it's frustrating for the parent and often devastating for the child, in terms of self-confidence/self-worth etc, while a more fiery child will be able to stand up to the parents.

If there were two children and one parent was fiery and the other watery, then it's likely that one child would be more fiery and the other more watery. If the parents are balanced, then provided they were relatively balanced when the children were born and raised, the children should follow suit.

In the case of two watery parents, at least one of the children will be more fiery, with a result that they will do whatever they can to get some feeling of security/firm boundary from their parents. When they don't get it, they will be driven to do whatever it takes to try to get some firm response, which may see the rebel emerge in them.

How fiery/watery are you?

Answer the questions below to gain insight into how watery or fiery you are.

Answer yes or no to the following questions:

1. I tend to always initiate social outings etc in my relationships.
2. I am always busy and seldom find time for myself.
3. I procrastinate often.
4. I tend to initiate sex more often in my relationship.
5. I avoid conflict whenever possible
6. I smoke regularly
7. I am very ambitious
8. I am happy with what I have
9. I would rather have less and enjoy the company of friends/family that have more and see less of them.
10. I enjoy water sports which give me a thrill such as surf-sailing, river rafting, surfing etc.
11. I start things but seldom finish them
12. My favourite place to be would be out in the bushveld watching wild animals.
13. Do you tend to always show the most initiative at work?
14. Are you afraid to make decisions?
15. Do you naturally take the lead?
16. Are you quick to anger?

If you answered yes to questions 1, 2, 4, 7, 10, 13, 15, 16 then chances are you are more fiery than if you answered yes to 3, 5, 6, 8, 9, 11, 12, 14, which would indicate you are more watery.

Fire and water in the bedroom

What happens when extreme fire, meets extreme water in the bedroom?

Take Dave and Cathy. Dave is a musical boffin and very watery. Cathy is an Accounts Director and very fiery. Cathy's life is all about doing – she gets out there, she goes after accounts, she is relentlessly driven and some may call her a workaholic. In the beginning she was drawn to Dave, because she felt a calm reassurance being in his company. She saw in his manner a silent strength. He enjoyed her for her intellectual stimulation and felt energised and reassured by her ability to cope with any and every situation.

While he sat composing his latest piece (which could take days, even weeks) and may require hours of research, contemplation and just generally hanging around waiting for inspiration, Cathy would be out on the streets actively pursuing a potential client or managing a new campaign. Over time however, what had been appealing, became a major source of irritation to both parties. Cathy was driven to distraction by his lack of doing, which also included paying the bills and general house management, such as packing the dishwasher and making the bed. His ability to distance himself from the day to day issues, made her feel alone and overburdened by the running of their affairs. He meanwhile, was resentful towards her, feeling constantly that she put everything, in particular work, well ahead of himself. He felt like an accessory to her busy schedule and not an integrated and meaningful part of her life.

What happened in the bedroom over time was that withdrawal on his part (as a disempowered attempt to maintain control of her) meant he would not, no matter how aroused he felt initiate sex. It wasn't that he didn't want to have sex, he just didn't want to be the one who initiated it, for fear no doubt that he would be as rejected in the bedroom as he felt rejected by her constant busy-ness in their life.

She however, was expectant in wanting him to display, at least in this area, a bit more fire, while he, tired of her fiery activity wanted her to be more watery. The result was a stalemate, which, in an attempt not to expose their vulnerability to each other, remained a taboo subject.

With her fire not being able to be joined with his water the situation would either become overtly watery – passive hostility, sulking and withdrawal on both sides or become too fiery – meaning that it would become a series of arguments, criticisms and possibly even abusive.

In this situation silent resentment grew on both sides. In moments of extreme resentment, he became in her mind the "arsehole," while she became the "frigid bitch," in his.

When male and female energies have sex, not only is it a pleasurable and fun, but energetically it provides an opportunity for balance to take place, which is why commonly men collapse into a relaxed sleep after sex, having become more watery/passive and women tend to want to become more active (fiery).

It is as a result of this balance seeking mechanism of fire/water that sex has so many positive attributes, from de-stressing, increased happiness, to enhancing the immune system, longevity, reduction in the occurrence of heart disease, prostrate problems and pain management.[1] When we are in balance we are all of these things and the more out of balance we are, the more we become the opposite i.e. depressed, with weakened immune systems, stressed and unhappy.

In spite of this, Western religion has frequently sought to portray sex as a sin with horrendous results such as HIV Aids, unwanted pregnancies, rape and harmful perversions and in so doing, override the positive effects of sex.

If one is not in balance and you are for whatever reason unable to have sex and the idea of masturbation is not an option for you, then chances are that this will create tension within you and possibly in your relationships. Orgasm releases oxytocin. Higher levels of oxytocin in the body has been shown to reduce the level of stress we experience, as well as creating feelings of warmth and affection for our partners. This is why after sex we are more loving and tolerant towards our partner, whereas beforehand we might have been irritated by them. Which is why sex is such an important part of our relationship – it helps us get through those bad times.

When someone is depressed their libido usually fades – they become so watery (tearful, not able to act, withdrawn etc.) that they have no fire to desire to do anything least of all have sex. One of the downfalls of many antidepressants is a reduced desire for sex, so while the antidepressant may manage to counter some of the symptoms of depression, it may do so at the expense of our sexual drive.

Getting back to Dave and Cathy, how can the relationship and balance be restored? Cathy will have to learn to be more receiving (watery) and thus allow Dave to give more (fire). This shift in power, will mean he will naturally have to respond by taking a more pro-active dominant role. She will have to empower him and criticise and attempt to dominate less, so that he feels in charge and consequently less likely to need to withdraw as a means of attempting to dominate passively. One might argue as to why she would have to be the one to act in their relationship and make the initial change, and the answer would be that it is not so much a male/female thing, but rather that the more fiery of the two will be more equipped to take the first step to change. Fire after all is the element aligned with change.

As one person changes in the relationship, so it will necessitate a change in the behaviour of the other person – that's how fire and water interact.

Any Dominatrix (a woman who acts out the role of a domineering partner in a sado-masochistic relationship often professionally) will tell you that their partners are most often men who have reached a degree of external power in the world. By that I mean they are often C.E.O.'s, M.D.'s and high powered business men. They have so much power in fact that in order to bring themselves into balance they seek out women who humiliate them and make them feel helpless by tying them up, disciplining them, (often with whips etc) verbally abusing them and forcing them into submission. This is an extreme form of the fiery male, seeking out a fiery woman to reduce him to submissive water.

Massage with fire and rain

If you are the sort of person who is very fiery – always on the go, battling to sit still etc then the chances are that when you go for a massage, it would be most beneficial to you to have either a massage which is slow and gentle or something such as Reiki where movement is limited or completely still. This will help bring you into balance. If on the other hand you are very watery – you battle to get things done or motivate yourself and feel low on energy, then a more vigorous approach would be helpful. Experiment with both types of treatments and see what effect each has on you.

Holiday with Fire and Rain

What do most people dream of when it comes to going on a relaxing holiday?

Going to a tropical island or Mediterranean paradise, a beach holiday or skiing perhaps? Working with the principles of Fire and Water, it's easy to understand why. All the time spent in fiery activity, needs balancing and where better than somewhere with lots of water (or frozen water i.e. snow). Surfers are known for their laid back approach to life. Why?. . . because they spend so much time in water.

What about gay relationships?

In any relationship the principle of a balance between fire and water energies remains the same. It does not matter if your partner is the same sex as you are. Your actual sex is of little consequence, it's more about the amount of fire/water each individual has. In any relationship, one person tends to take the lead in certain areas, while the other waits to be led. Sometimes this can fluctuate, however the predominance of fire usually falls to one person, while the passivity of water remains with the other.

What happens when you cannot, for whatever reason have a partner?

Your ability to be whole does not rest with another, any more than your ability to be happy does. Balance comes from within. There are many theories from an astrological and karmic point of view as to why one person has no relationships while another has many. Looks are often used as the reason, but I have known many good-looking people who have struggled to find relationships, while people who are not gifted with looks, often have many relationships. So simply being good-looking is not a guarantee of finding happiness in relationships – just read the tabloids to see how unhappy most superstars (who usually have looks on their side, are). Perhaps right now in your life, it may be a time to work with finding your own inner balance, which will certainly assist any future relationship to be more fulfilling.

Note

1. Although a causal relationship has yet to be demonstrated, a U.S. survey of nearly 3,500 women and men showed that personal happiness is associated with the frequency of sexual activity and orgasm — especially among women (Laumann, *et al.*, 1994) and may be associated with reducing the risk of the two leading causes of death in the U.S.A. – heart disease and cancer. (Ebrahim, *et al.*, 2002; Petridou, *et al.*, 2000).
   Published: 04.04.03 |
   From: The Health Benefits of Sexual Expression
   http://www.plannedparenthood.org/news-articles-press/politics-policy-issues/medical-sexual-health/The-Health-Benefits-of-Sexual-Expression.htm 30 April 2007

Chapter Four

Archetypes

What are they?

W hen our relationships are not fulfilling and in balance, we will encounter the negative aspects of our archetypes.

What does this mean? And what actually is an archetype?

The word archetype comes originally from the Latin word *archetypum* from the Greek word *arkhetypon* meaning *arkhe* – first or original and *typos* meaning type or model. So the word itself meant first type or original mould. It was used in the 1500's and was not, as many conclude, a word created by Swiss psychiatrist Carl Jung, rather he coined the word to describe an image that arose from our collective unconscious in the 1900's.

What Jung realised was that there were certain characters if you like, that resided within our group psyches, which we act out, both as people internally but also externally in our books, fairytales, folklore, legends, plays, films, advertising and groups, and in the case of the Greeks and many primal people as our gods.

These archetypes then predetermine a type of behaviour or personality we can expect. For instance if someone describes a friend as a "computer nerd," we have a pretty clear idea, not only of what the person looks like, but also the sort of behaviour we can expect from him. It's a stereotype of a person and their attributes. So from the term a "Prima Donna," we know we can expect a large ego and petulant self-centred outbursts, while from a "knight in shinning armour," we know we have a man who loves rescuing damsels in distress. A "real bastard," does not relate now to someone's lack of a father, but more to a man who acts meanly and without conscience, to the detriment of others.

These archetypical patterns are woven into the fabric of our lives and we use them constantly, often without really realising we are doing so. (Think how many times you use the terms" couch potato," "real princess," "hippy," "earth mother," "arsehole," "sugar daddy," etc. Even certain jobs carry with them societies' concepts of certain character types, such as "second hand car salesman," "executive," "fashion model," and so on. Through these descriptions we get an idea of the type of person we are speaking about and their motivations for behaving the way they do.

An interesting look at the sound of the word "archetype."

(Pronounced "R key type".)

Often words when broken down into auditory segments, reveal a deeper meaning such as (w) hol (y) ness, dis-ease (not at ease), busyness (business keeps us busy) etc.

The che in the word is a transliteration of the Greek word chi (pronounced "key"). This is interesting because the word chi (or ki in Japanese), is used to describe universal energy or life force. (It's found in words like Reiki, a form of alternative balancing/healing). So taking the word "ki/chi/che," we can see that are che types. In other words different ways of expressing universal energy or life force within us, through these different roles we assume.

Are (our) che (energy) types

There are any numbers of archetypes, however the four Jung focused on primarily, were the anima (the female aspect of ourselves which in this book is represented by the element of water), the male aspect of ourselves or animus, which in this book is represented by the element of fire, the self, which our whole or holy self, represented often by a circle. This is when we have integrated all aspects of our personality, including our shadow self, which is the fourth archetype, he commonly refers to.

Each of us have a number of different archetypes that we use. At certain times in our lives, we may be drawn to certain archetypes more than others, or we may outgrow the need for some along the way, as we adopt others. We may also choose to work through the darker aspects of an archetype or move into its more positive expression.

In Jungian psychology, this "shadow," represents aspects of ourselves that are hidden or repressed as well as weaknesses and instincts we would rather disown. Others may see and recognize them, but we ourselves don't, as they form part of our subconscious mind. The more we disown our shadow, the larger it becomes. Take the analogy of a see-saw. When we are in the centre, we are in balance, and have integrated all aspects of ourselves. The greater our shadow, the more the see-saw will swing out of balance and into experiencing life and relationships as traumatically up and down.

There is often the mistaken belief that only "bad" aspects are in the shadow, but this is not so. We may have always wanted to be an artist, but were ridiculed as a child for this interest. Now it resides in our shadow. Part of our healing would involve connecting with this aspect of ourselves and exploring this inner suppressed artist to bring it from the shadow into the light. As such it becomes an exciting journey of self-discovery. Jung himself acknowledged that the shadow may be irrational and appear instinctively, but that this did not mean it was evil as such. Sometime we may find someone close or even ourselves, acts completely out of character (or so it seems) which may be confusing. The chances are that this is our shadow self emerging.

I recall many years ago a friend's husband, who was normally a very serious sort of chap, (while she was a wildly extrovert party-goer), after a few drinks started doing a strip for everyone complete with wild hip gyrations etc. We were completely taken aback. This was just not the man we knew.

Can you see the dynamic between the two?

What happened was that in his shadow self, was the woman he had married, namely the wild party-goer. He had kept this aspect of himself suppressed his whole life, most likely because he had learnt from a young age that such behavior was simply "not nice!" A few drinks had loosened this control and "bang" out popped his shadow wild party man.

Drink and drugs often are very relevant or instigational in letting our shadows surface. Which is why the quiet shy guy becomes hugely aggressive or the demure secretary becomes a wild flirt at the office party.

I recall in South Africa during the years of apartheid rule when relations across races were banned, how often one would read of a dominee (note resemblance to the word "dominate"!) a minister of the Afrikaans Dutch Reformed church, being caught in a "location" (areas where black people were allocated to live) or across the border in a neighboring state, having sex with one of the local black people. The strict repression that he lived in, would surface in shadow behavior that was considered a huge scandal in his community and congregation.

Exercise:
1. Get a notepad
2. Give yourself at least ten minutes uninterrupted time.
3. Now write down all the things you dislike in others, such as cruelty, selfishness etc.

Be as specific as you can. (We'll refer back to this exercise later)

Whatever we repress, gets expressed through our shadow selves in our archetypes.

The archetypes or their opposites then are the chi or energy vehicle that we use to express what is in our shadow selves. We then take this shadow self and project it on another person and they then become the enemy, the enemy as Jung says, that is really within ourselves. The more we find fault with others, the more we constrict ourselves and reduce our self worth. In accepting others, we in reality accept ourselves – warts and all. So a personal imbalance is projected onto our partner or someone else. The more we dislike others and judge them, indicates just how much we dislike ourselves, because all the so called "faults" in them we pick up on, deep down we recognize them in ourselves. Whatever angers you about another, whatever you find distasteful, horrific or unpleasant, resides within your shadow.

That's a tough one to have to deal with!

You may have been in a situation where a friend is discussing a colleague or another person familiar to you and they mention certain behaviors they find offensive about that person. You think about it and are surprised as these behaviors don't worry you – you may not even be aware of them. What's happened then, is that these actions push your friend's buttons, but because you don't have those aspects in your shadow, they don't push your buttons.

By recognizing your archetypes you can,

- recognize their opposites in your partner
- balance the conflicting energies within yourself
- (which will) change the dynamics of the relationship

By recognizing the darker aspects of our shadow selves through our archetypes and balancing these, we lose the fear of what others will think of us. Why? Simply because when we worry about what others will think of us, we are afraid deep down that they will see into our shadow selves. By enlightening ourselves about our shadow aspects, the shadow no longer holds fear for us. What was in the dark is now in the light. Truly great people have lost all fear of what others will think, because through integrating their shadow into the Self, they have nothing to fear in terms of what could be exposed – they have faced their demons and dealt with them.

To grow and become whole, we have to face a variety of archetypes within ourselves: the Miser, the Control Freak, the Drama Queen, the Victim and so on. This does not mean that you are a drama queen as such all the time, just that you have the potential to be one. That is why this work is so hard. It's much nicer falling in love with our own perceived "positive" aspects than having to confront the nasty bits!

Phillip Zimbardo, a psychologist professor emeritus at Stanford University in the *Stanford Prison Experiment*, did a radical experiment to show just how true this is. Recruiting 24 well adjusted healthy middle class students, he created a mock prison in the university. Randomly dividing the men into prisoners and wardens by the toss of a coin, he observed how each group adapted to its role, way beyond his expectations. The so called "guards" started behaving cruelly to the point that a third of them were found to be exhibiting authentic sadistic behavior, while the "prisoners," after a brief rebellion, started becoming severely traumatized to the point that he had to terminate the experiment. It produced shocking results, but did provide real proof of the fact that within our shadow we can find, under pressure, aspects of ourselves we may never have suspected existed. (Similar experiments were then held at other universities and showed similar results.)

Soldiers in wars, experience these same phenomena, as many films about Vietnam have shown. Acting against ones understanding of what constitutes correct behavior is a major problem when it comes to having to readapt to "normal" life.

The reason why horror movies and TV crime stories fascinate, is that we can observe our shadow selves as the villains in the drama, without having to admit their existence within ourselves. Fairy Tales also have these opposing archetypes, (see my previous book, *Climbing the Beanstalk*) such as the sweet beauty of Cinderella contrasted with the ugly cruelty of her stepsisters and mother, or Beauty contrasted with the Beast.

While projecting one archetype onto another, the opposite archetype will live within us. So if we are the child in a relationship and project the role of critical and controlling parent onto our partner, then within our own shadow is the critical parent.

To become integrated or whole then entails acknowledging and accepting all aspects of the shadow and in so doing we replace judgment of ourselves and others, with love – we see the Divine spark or potential in each person we meet, which is the habit of all great men and women (and the need to project falls away).

Exercise: Get that list you wrote earlier when you wrote down all the attributes you least liked in others. Read through it. It should give you an indication as to what's lurking in your Shadow.

Why we play archetypal roles

When we create opposite archetypes in relationships there is always a payoff or benefit of some sort to ourselves. Now this may seem hard to swallow if you are playing the role of the Victim for instance; and you may ask what possible benefit there could be in that, however if you really look honestly at yourself you will always find some payback, otherwise you would not have stuck with the role as long as you have. This is a hard thing to do and you will have to fight your ego along the way, who will not want you to accept responsibility for your behavior.

However, if you really want to alter the dynamic of your relationship, a bit of self-examination is essential.

In each of the archetypal roles in Section Two are clues to assist you in this journey of self-discovery. If while reading these it causes a strong reaction in you (most often along the lines of "that's rubbish, I'm not....") then know that you may have hit upon your payoff.

For instance, let's take the Victim archetype. In her book *Why People Don't Heal And How They Can,* author Caroline Myss spends some time with the Victim archetype and suggests that the payoff for the victim is attention currency – that often we may enjoy the attention we demand from others when we talk about our wounds. To let go of the wound means to let go of what allows us to get input from others. We all desire attention and its understandable then why it may be hard to give up something that serves to provide it, even if doing so holds us as a victim. By understanding what the payoff is for you in the archetypal role you are playing, you not only raise your consciousness, but take a huge step towards balancing the opposite archetypes within yourself and your relationship.

These roles we play are just that. They are not who we really are, but what we assume in order to learn. Just like an actor who plays a part, he is not the part, and neither are we our archetypes.

What if my partner doesn't want to change?

Even if our partner is not interested in changing, if we change, we alter the dynamic of the relationship which will inevitably have a knock-on effect on our partner.

Because the role they are playing for us is a projection of the opposite role that we are playing we only have to change for the complete dynamic of the relationship to change.

An adult assuming the fearful and irresponsible Child archetype, cannot act the Child if the critical Parent is absent, while a hen-pecked husband, requires a dominant woman to do the pecking. Likewise the critical Parent needs a Child to criticize. It does as they say, take two to tango.

Nothing in the Universe happens without it affecting the world around us. Today a truck rolled on the N1. It affected the truck driver for sure, but it also affected all the rush hour commuters who were up to two hours later than normal for work. This in turn affected people who they were due to have appointments with, company production and so on. This in turn may have affected delivery orders, which now could affect people overseas who had never heard about the truck-drivers crash and so on. You cannot act alone. Someone (and usually many people) will be affected by your actions.

In order to stop the game of opposite archetypes you will need to:

- Recognize (name) the archetypes in the relationship,
- See who is who
- Identify the archetypes your partner has and their opposites in you
- See what the payoff is for yourself
- Work to balance the archetype you show and the one you conceal in your shadow through this awareness by asking the question: Do I want to remain see-sawing between these archetypal roles or do I want to bring myself and my relationship into balance?"

It's hard to assume the role of the change maker, but it may be harder still to remain locked into a relationship that is not spontaneous, uplifting and intimate.

Change and you

As you read through this book, you may recognise your own archetypal patterns and their mirror in your partner. It can be unpleasant to have to face the fact that you are playing for instance, the role of a Tyrant or Victim. Remember though that we all play various roles. Through recognizing the archetypes you have taken a major step into transforming them.

The universe is in a constant state of change. So to change is natural, whereas we often regard it as unnatural – some sort of force to be defied and resisted. There is no person who is not capable of change on some level - even if your relationship seems impossible. Through your changing, you ignite the fire of change in the world and people around you, (whether they know it or not.)

We cannot fight change, rather we can embrace it and work with it to transform and uplift ourselves.

That is self-mastery.

Are all archetypes "bad"?

Archetypes have two aspects to them. For instance a rebel when worked with in the positive side, will help us rebel against religious systems that no longer serve us, beliefs that are constricting or corporate thinking that is not enhancing the growth of the company or that is detrimental to the environment. In the negative side, the rebel may spur us to rebel against our parents, simply to look cool to our peers. It may, have us dress and act outrageously, more as an act of the ego than upliftment of self. A Parent archetype is necessary when raising children or looking after an elderly invalid friend or parent for example, however, and in this instance is nurturing and encouraging, while in the negative, the Parent is critical, controlling and domineering.

Positive aspects of archetypes are seldom those that present difficulties in our lives – it's the more shadow aspects that cause friction and upset in relationships. Consequently the archetypes worked with in the book, are these negative or shadow archetypes, because in bringing them out of the shadow and into the light we ourselves become more enlightened.

Chapter Five

The See-saw Scenario

If I'm up why does he bring me down?

Imagine a see-saw where the fulcrum represents an emotional wound and either end of the seesaw and the way it tips, how the wound expresses itself.

If the wound is for example "inadequacy," it may express itself by having a bully archetype at the one end and a victim at the other. So the bully and the victim both carry the same wound which expresses itself through different archetypal responses, by attempting to inflate or deflate, in order to work through the wound, come into the centre of the see-saw and transform the wound.

You're on cloud nine. You're hip and hop and happening. Business is booming, your boss loves your ideas, you've just won a big contract, promotion is being spoken about, you're feeling great and you burst through the door exuding frivolity and enthusiasm, only to encounter your partner who clearly has not been having as good a day. Storm clouds swirl around his head and his sarcastic reply crashes you back to earth. What is happening?

Your euphoric mood put you at the top of the see-saw. Your partner's mood is angry and depressed and consequently weighing you down. His response makes you come crashing down. Now there are two people who are not feeling good. Worse still, you each blame the other person for how you are feeling, or the situation you are in.

If you imagine two plastic bottles with a pipe going from the one's opening to the other's, if one were to contain water, as you heated this water up it would boil and the pressure would cause air to rise through the tube and into the other container increasing pressure there.

If you are in a bad mood, then using our example of the two plastic bottles, the heat in your bottle will rise and create pressure in the other bottle. That's what happens in relationships. People do not act in an isolated manner. What happens to you affects those around you and vice-versa.

If one partner is heavy with emotional baggage and feeling down, the last thing they want is their partner floating high and en-lightened. Naturally, in an attempt to reach balance they will attempt to bring their partner down. If you're up, you naturally want your partner to be up too. Only trying to lift him/her inevitably means you tend to slide downwards. We want those around us to suffer, as we are making ourselves suffer.

Have you ever sat in a group where the conversation turned to the amount of crime around? As each nasty tale is told, the stories become more terrifying in order to outdo the previous story. By the end of the chat, everyone is feeling afraid or at least nervous and untrusting. Even when people talk about a subject which should be uplifting, such as childbirth, the stories tend to go from one horror episiotomy to the next forty-nine hour labour with no pain relief.

Bringing others down in this manner, is a natural tendency for our lower selves which thrives on pain. Why do the media, proportionally, cover more bad news than good? Because our lower selves love misery, corruption and general bad news. Listening to the unfortunate events around us, makes us feel less bad about our own pain and traps us into a cycle of belief that pain is our natural state of being.

I worked freelance for a local newspaper a number of years ago. My payment per story was directly related to its sensational (read pain) content. The more angst and drama, the bigger my fee. While not all media work on this principle consciously, I suspect the rule still applies even if it is subconscious. We love magazines that gossip about celebrities and their antics because they maintain this illusion that unhappiness/drama etc is the way to be. We (or rather our lower ego-based selves), feeds off the negativity of others, just as we hover around a crash site hoping for a glimpse of carnage. The movie producers are aware of this and dish out any number of films which delight our lower selves and mean that we, as a race don't feel inclined to move beyond this attraction to pain and disaster.

Our one to one relationships are often no different and we thrive on creating drama that gets us attention from others and verifies the misguided belief that we are all intrinsically victims of circumstances beyond our control. (And with this thinking we are).

The general tendency then is to bring the other person down to our level, rather than ask them to lift us up to theirs.

The universe as a balance seeking mechanism

The Golden Mean was discovered by Leonardo Pisano Fibonacci who was born in Italy in 1170. Although he travelled widely, (he sometimes referred to himself as a Bigollo, meaning a traveller). He was by nature an extremely clever mathematician. Amongst other things, he discovered the Golden Mean/Section which is also known as the Fibonacci Series. It consists of a series of numbers, each number being the addition of the two previous numbers: 1, 1, 2, 3, 5, 8, 13, 21, 34, 55, 89, 144 and so on. (1+1=2, 2+1=3, 2+3=5...). What becomes interesting is when you start dividing the previous number into the one ahead of it. At around 144 the results start becoming consistent and continue ad infinitum at the ratio of 1:618 or roughly 60/40.)

You will find this sequence or its ratio, in many things in nature, such as the quantity of male (drones) to female bees, the proportion of the body structure of creatures from dolphins to tigers, penguins to ants, to the markings on butterflies: from pineapple skin formation to shells, from the music of Mozart, to the works of Leonardo da Vinci the pyramids, the human body, the ark of the covenant, credit cards, sunflowers, the galaxy and even in the prediction of population growth of various cities. And being an imprint of our own physical bodies, it is also an imprint for our energetic ones. (From the feet to the navel = 60% of average person's height. Divide the remaining 40% of the height into 60/40 and you'll be left with the head as 40%. Take the head and do the same and you'll divide on the line of the eyes and so on. The same works for the fingers and hand).

Whatever you may ask has this little mathematical interlude to do with you and your difficult partner? The answer is plenty. If we take this pattern from the physical structure of our bodies and apply it to the mental/emotional aspects of ourselves, we'll see then that the ideal balance of fire and water in ourselves is not 50/50, but rather 60/40.

For ourselves to be in balance then we will need to carry 60% male or female energy with the balance making up the 40% and if we have a partner then they would need to complement that in reverse. This means that a man who is out of touch or who has suppressed his feminine side will be out of balance, just as a woman who is afraid to express her masculine side will be.

If your own male and female aspects are not in balance, then you will attract a similar partner, most likely with the opposite imbalance. This, in the case of a man who is for example 80% in his male aspect and suppressing his 20% female, will result in a man who is authoritarian (my way is THE WAY), domineering (the belief that women are somehow second class citizens/colleagues etc) has rigid boundaries and is very controlling. Aspects of the feminine, such as compliancy, receptiveness to others, feelings, nurturing, gentleness, expressing emotions etc will be suppressed, and often scorned as being weak. These men will often mock men who are gay, yet may often have repressed homosexual sexual desires. Why is this?

Simply because in repressing their feminine in their shadow side, aspects of their own femine nature which includes attraction to men, have been suppressed. Should the desire emerge, it is so unacceptable to this man who has to project a macho man image to the world that he ridicules what he fears the most – his own repressed feminine self. If such a man were to enter into a relationship with a woman, who was also male dominant in a similar way, the result would be explosive – two fires making an enormous blaze which would burn out fast with neither getting their needs met! If his present partner started to grow her masculine side, he would feel threatened and probably ridicule her attempts to do so, leaving her angry and frustrated.

Chances are though, that a man who had completely suppressed his feminine side, would be attracted to a woman who had suppressed her male aspects and had overly compensated with her feminine side. This would make her compliant to the point of being submissive, having no boundaries and little self esteem. He could then order her around, often resulting in abuse, without fearing that he would meet any significant resistance. To come into balance, he would need to connect with his female side and work at incorporating these aspects into his psyche, which would mean he would become comfortable with his feminine nature.

Unfortunately for most men in this category, the fear of doing this supersedes the desire to heal themselves and their relationships. Often healing has to evolve through the female becoming more empowered and working at releasing her inner suppressed male, so that she learns to stand up for herself.

The woman in this relationship often has an idealised distorted view of what being a woman entails. In her desire to match up to his machismo, if he is a "mans' man," she must be a girlie girl. She may come to believe that things such as wearing make-up 24/7, pouting bo-toxed lips, spending a small fortune on the latest fashions, having cosmetic surgery to get the perfect body/face, dressing alluringly or wearing sprays that destroy a natural woman's smell, are what constitute being a woman. She has lost connection with her inner true feminine nature and opted for a Hollywood version, which being fantasy, she never can quite fulfil, leaving her feeling a failure.

What happens in the opposite relationship that is out of balance, i.e. where the male is 80% into his feminine side and his male is suppressed, while his female partner is 80% male? As the domineering party, the woman, will most likely take the lead in earning capacity and even if this is not the case, may treat the man with contempt. She did not plan to marry a drip (water) she wanted a real man? Why? So that she would be able to release her fear of expressing her feminine side. The feeling being "only if I have a real man, can I be a real woman." Until then I have to (resentfully), assume the role. Frequently the man will be hen-pecked - remember Mrs. Bucket (pronounced at her insistence as "Bouquet") in the BBC TV series *Keeping up Appearances*? As her frustration grows, so does his inadequacy and so the situation worsens, to the point that he withdraws emotionally into a passive aggressive space, so that there is absolutely no intimacy or real communication.

After such a relationship and with his inner male unhealed, if left he may be persuaded to go for the polar opposite woman – namely a woman who is equally as watery. The result will be a relationship where neither needs are met – there is too little fire resulting in no boundaries, little discipline, no routine, probably financial problems and little or no structure.

Remember the days of the hippies, when men started wearing flowers, growing their hair long and smoking weed, which made them very laid back and passive (more into their feminine side). What was the result? Undisciplined children, undisciplined sexual expression (no boundaries/free love), little money and a general watery laid back lifestyle. This was in complete contrast to the previous generation, where the male aspects were overemphasized and men were "The Boss" and women their second class, compliant helpers.

From a book entitled: "Fascinating Womanhood," by Helen B. Andelin[1]

Do's

Admire the manly things about him.

Recognize his superior strength and ability

Be a Domestic Goddess.

Revere your husband and honor his right to rule you and your children.

Don't's

Don't show indifference, contempt, or ridicule towards his masculine abilities, achievements or ideas.

Don't try to excel him in anything which requires masculine ability.

Don't let the outside world crowd you for time to do your homemaking tasks well.

Don't stand in the way of his decisions, or his law.

It's easy to understand then why there was an imbalance and why it resulted in the era of the hippies. You can see then that there was a polar shift from one generation where the male was too fiery, to the following one where he rebelled against the fire and went in the opposite watery direction. (After which we all scuttled back into high powered corporations from which we are now trying to extract ourselves to look for more "quality" of life!)

In a balanced relationship where male/female is around 60/40 in either direction, the man will be able to assume a feminine role whenever the situation calls for it, such as happily nurturing children - cooking, collecting, changing etc,

[1] *Fascinating Womanhood*, by Helen B. Andelin Pacific Press, Santa Barbara, 1963.

while the woman will be able to step into a male role such as earning a living for the family should the need arise. In this relationship, choices are made together and each partner acknowledges what the other brings to the relationship. There is complete acceptance, freedom, giving and receiving flow freely and spontaneity and playfulness exist in the relationship, which is fulfilling to both parties.

We know that after wars when many more men have been killed, there is an increase in the number of male babies born, as nature seeks to rectify the imbalance. This same need to rectify the imbalance is expressed in ourselves when we are out of balance. Relationships then are our way of trying to find balance, which is why they are so popular!

The fifty/fifty myth

All men are not equal.

Some men (and women) are more equal than others. Not all men (and women) have equal beauty, height, intelligence, wealth, weight and talent:

Why then do we expect our relationships to be about fifty/fifty?

- If I wash the dishes/cook three nights a week, you must do the same and we'll eat out or negotiate the remaining night.
- If I spend three hours looking after junior, then you must do the same.
- If I mow the lawn this week, then it's your turn next week.
- You make the bed today and I'll make it tomorrow?
- You must match what I earn.

Does your relationship manage to adhere long term to rules like these?

If it does it's unusual, because rules like these don't allow for the fact that some people are better at and enjoy different tasks. (Also in some relationships one person makes the other feel so useless that they don't do an activity, because doing so means that they will inevitably fail in their partner's eyes.) Equality then needs to be closer to the Golden Mean, if it is to work.

You may initiate sex more often than I do, however if I never initiate sex that may be a problem for you, because no-one wants to feel 100% responsible all of the time for love-making. By working in the 40/60 framework, we can find a balance that suits your partner's needs and yours. This paradigm also gets rid of the need for competition between partners, which can be very destructive. Accepting each others strengths and weaknesses is going to go a long way to further a relationship.

The relationship bank

This Golden Mean spills over into what we give and take in a relationship. Most people when asked, will feel that they give more than they receive in a relationship.

This is still ok as long as it doesn't get beyond the 60% mark. After that resentment will result. And the relationship will deteriorate. Obviously there are times, such as when one person is ill, that one does do more giving, but as a general rule a relationship is like a bank account. What you put in, you expect to withdraw.

He may give more financially, she may give more emotionally. He may withdraw more emotional support, while she may spend more, but overall giving and receiving are between 40 and 60%. Many people find it difficult to receive and hold the belief that somehow it's more noble to give than to receive. However, for many people giving is a pleasure. By not allowing another to give, we withhold their ability to experience that pleasure. Giving is, in principle, a male act, while in receiving we experience feminine surrender. To be in balance we need to be able to do both.

In the workshops I run, one exercise would test by using the body (the body doesn't lie) as a means to determine whether the individual found giving easier or more difficult. On very few occasions did anyone find it easier to receive.

If we keep the analogy of the bank in mind then, we can see how it is essential to not only put into our relationship bank, but also to allow ourselves to withdraw such things as energy, finance, love, support, time etc when the need arises.

When relationships choices can become more out of balance, the more out of balance we become.

Not only can relationships assist us to come into a greater degree of balance through seeing our projections in our partners, but they can also regress if we don't work at doing so. Here is a rather sad example of just that:

Neilia, started off in a reasonably balanced relationship. Errol was watery, while she was the more fiery partner. He was a kind and loving man and a devoted partner. In time, this frustrated her and she developed a wandering eye (and body!) Life with him just wasn't exciting enough. Eventually she ended their relationship.

Errol moved on and up in the world. Neilia however, had a series of unhappy liaisons. Eventually she entered into a more serious relationship and had a child. This man was supposedly what she had wanted - a hot-headed game ranger and very much a man's man. She had become depressed (water) and so attracted him (fire). At first she had enjoyed the way he took over and assumed control. He was so" manly." However, a few months down the road and this attribute had become stifling, dominating and suppressive, leading to the end of the relationship.

She had started to become more unbalanced and this was mirrored by her following choice of partner, who amongst other peculiarities, refused to have sex with her, considering it immoral while at the same time refusing to marry her.

Rather than be pleased by his stoic stand, she felt that he was rejecting her femininity and feeling that the relationship was futile moved on.

Her desperation to find another partner was increasing with each failed relationship and her choice of partners became more and more unbalanced, as she herself became more unbalanced. Her need for a partner became so extreme, that she was charged with office harassment, when she tried to blackmail a colleague into having a relationship with her.

She found her next choice of partner on an Internet dating site. He seemed the answer to her prayers. However, in time it became apparent that he had created a series of lies about his past and that he was not what he appeared to be. His behaviour showed all the characteristics of being a sociopath, in his lying, his lack of conscience, his abusive episodes, his desire to do very little and feed off her income, the way he shifted from throwing violent tantrums when confronted, to making her feel sorry for him and thus being highly manipulative.

In the year they were married, he ran rip-shod through her life. At this point she had hit her lowest ebb. Although those who are unfortunate enough to find themselves in relationships with sociopaths are not necessarily unbalanced, in Neilia's case, it was an indication of how unbalanced she had become.

The point of telling this story, is not to go into the voyeuristic details of someone else's fall into despair, but rather to demonstrate how we repeat patterns through our choices of partners, becoming more and more unbalanced with each new relationship. Likewise, we can reverse the situation through inner balancing and becoming aware of our own energies, so we can attract more balanced relationships into our lives.

Out of balance

A friend's husband was driving home from work when a car pulled out right in front of him. To avoid a collision he swung hard off the road and into the bushes. The other driver, swerved onto the opposite verge. He glared across the road at the driver - a woman with two small children, but she barely heeded him, as she put the accelerator down and turned across the road, intending to go in the opposite direction. She did not look down the road and consequently did not see the large van cruising towards her. When she turned at point blank range in front of the van, it hit her full on, crushing her small car and injuring her severely. (The children were not physically harmed.)

It transpired that she had had an argument with her boyfriend, who had driven off and she was attempting to chase him. (He, by now far down the road, was oblivious to the chaos behind him). This woman was clearly swinging way out of balance and behaving irrationally as a result.

The more out of balance we are, the more chaos and unhappiness we create for ourselves.

This woman was so out of balance that she was prepared to risk her life and those of her children for an argument and as a result has had to endure painful surgery and handicaps that will remain with her for life. Life must be incredibly hard for her, harder still because her suffering is clearly as a direct result of her actions. (Although in this state of being, her boyfriend will bear the brunt of the blame.)

The same friend told me how that same morning, she saw a man driving his young daughter to school. Impatient in the heavy slow-moving traffic, he swerved across the road into the next lane and did not see an old man crossing the road. He knocked the man down. Instead though, of getting out of his car to help the man, he flung open the car door, made his way to the man (who was fortunately not badly hurt) and who was attempting to stand up. While his daughter watched, he punched him in the face, so hard the man once again was knocked to his feet, and this time was clearly hurt.

Imagine this child having to go to school and face a day of lessons after witnessing her father's behaviour. Here again is a man who is so unbalanced he cannot contain his fire. Once again imagine the trauma he will cause himself (not to mention the old man). Inevitably a car number will have been taken down, witnesses will testify as to his actions and he could land up in jail as a result. If he is not a sociopath, then later he will have to live with the guilt of his actions and the suffering they have caused another. As in the previous case though, he will in all likelihood, as a way to avoid these feelings, create the belief within himself that the old man was wrong, and that he was perfectly entitled to behave as he did, given the depth of wrongness of the old man.

While these examples are extreme, they are in the book to illustrate just how irrational our behaviour becomes the further away from our own centre we move – its not that unpleasant things won't occur when you are in balance, it's just that you won't keep creating *unnecessary* pain and trauma for yourself. And if you are in balance, your ability to recover from a painful situation will be much faster.

Balance and your diet

The more out of balance we are, the more out of balance our relationships will be and the more out of balance our diet will be (or vice-versa).

If you are out of balance, the chances are you'll be attracted to an unbalanced diet. Fast-foods, take-away burgers, fizzy drinks, processed foods, donuts etc will be what you desire. The more centred you become, the more you will be drawn to a balanced, healthy diet.

Chapter Six

The rest is history...

How our past determines our future

Not only do our life experiences shape our persona, but our parents play a very important role in determining the type of partner we will be attracted to (and the sort of partner we'll be.) I'm not talking about our parents arranging our marriages; I'm talking about an inner program that was written into our psyche way before we were even born.

It works like this:

Go back to your biology lessons and imagine a cell. A cell is made up of a membrane, a nucleus, and various other proteins and organelles. All of them moving around and doing their own thing supposedly, however they all make up the cell and its functioning. Take away one aspect away and it'll affect the whole cell. The cell membrane is permeable and in that way it can transfer particles to nearby cells. Imagine now that you are the nucleus of the cell and all the other bits represent various family members. What happens to each of them will affect you and vice-versa. The DNA in this cell is there because you inherited it from your parents, who inherited it from theirs and so on. What you inherited then, at its most basic level was their biology.

How you are physically, affects how you are emotionally. If you are tired and stressed emotionally, you are more likely to become physically ill. So this blue print that lives in our cells, also lives in our psyche. Each of the aspects of your cells moves and vibrates according to its history, just as you do and your DNA carries encoded into it certain dispositions to certain diseases.

Now here is the interesting part. If you cut your arm and have a few stitches it leaves a superficial scar on your skin. We have three primary layers of skin (with the exception of the palms and soles of the feet). The top layer, is called the epidermis. The epidermis is also composed of three layers. Each bottom layer works its way up to the surface of the skin where it is sloughed off. This process of the under layer of skin moving to the outer layer, takes a few weeks. So each external layer of skin is renewed within the space of a month. Why then does it keep making the same scar, if the original scar should have disappeared after a month? My son still has chicken pox scars on his back from when he had the illness 11 years ago. Why are they still there? Simply because the program has been written into his skin cells that keeps repeating itself, even though the original skin was lost about 132 sheddings ago.

What is true of our biology, is true of our lives as well. What has happened in the past and even before that in our family history, will repeat itself over and over again until we find a way to heal the scar and shed it forever. That's why working to understand your emotional issues is so awesome, because in letting go of these scars, you not only create a happier life for yourself, but you also heal the wound for your children, and their children and so on. So the whole cellular structure of the family improves just because of you!

Exercise (with thanks to Natalia Baker)
Look back in your family and see if you can pick up common themes that have repeated themselves over the generations. It may be alcoholism, certain illnesses, depression, a dominating father, irresponsibility, depression, lack of self worth, abusive behaviour or any other pattern you can see.

Note: You may do each of the three sections of this exercise separately, giving yourself time to process each section, or if you have the time, you may do the whole exercise in one period.

Give yourself at least an hour if you are going to do the total exercise in one go.

Part One

1. **Don't read through the complete exercise before you start doing it.** Read and do it step by step. Get a large sheet of paper and a pen.
2. Give yourself twenty minutes for this part of the exercise.
3. Write two headings at the top of your page: "Men" and "Women."
4. Write down all the words you can think of that relate to men and your experiences of them. This is free association, so write whatever comes into your head. It can be how you experience men, relationships you may have had with them, beliefs about men, and their role in your family, etc. Don't judge what you write; just write down whatever comes to mind. Some words could be: domineering, loving, providing, abusive, the boss etc

5. Then under the "women" heading, write down all the words that come to mind that relate to your experience of what a woman is. It can be how you experience women, how you feel as a woman, their role in your family, relationships you may have had with them etc.
6. Now take that piece of paper and underline the five words that jump out at you most under each list. (By this I mean selecting what words create more emotion in you as you read them.)
7. Now draw two circles:
8. Into the first circle put the five words from the first (men) list and into the second circle do the same for the female list, putting "men" above the male circle and "women" above the female circle.
9. Now look at the male list. See if you can see how it might mirror the relationship your father had towards your mother.
10. Now do the same for the female list in terms of what relationship your mother had with your father.
11. Spend at least 10 minutes reflecting on this relationship between your parents.

"YES BUT, what if it doesn't relate at all? I put cowardly under "men," but my father was actually a bully and abusive." Or, "I put selfish," where my experience of my mother was that she was generous." When you can identify an opposite behaviour, all that has happened is that in trying to balance this behaviour, you have experienced the opposite; the core issue however, remains the same wound. For example bullies often have a history of being bullied and a coward can often become a bully and vice-versa. Likewise someone may be generous with their money, but very selfish emotionally or alternatively selfish in thinking only of their own needs and using money as a way to manipulate others.

Part Two

12. Now below those two circles draw one circle and divide it vertically in two, putting the word "man" on the male side and "woman" on the female side.
13. Put your male and female words into this circle in their respective sides.
14. See this as being the circle representing you and your own inner male and female aspects. This may feel somewhat uncomfortable, but be open to what may be inside your shadow or hidden self.
15. Go through each word slowly and spend time on thinking about each one. Can you identify that behaviour within yourself? Or does the complete opposite apply?

Part Three

16. Draw a further two circles below the other three:
17. These two lower circles represent your relationships with males on the male side and females on the female side. If you look what's in your

man/woman aspects you will be able to see how you project these aspects or their opposites into the relationships you have with other men and women.

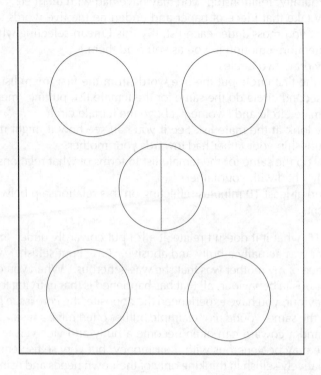

What the exercise shows us is that we energetically pick up the dynamics from our parents (who in turn picked them up from their parents and then continue to repeat the same energetic dynamics from one generation to the next, unless of course, we choose to alter the dynamics and **that's where you come in**.

You now, from what you have learnt in this exercise, have the power to choose what does not serve you and to do the work to make the appropriate changes.

Laura's chart looked like this:

Under the Male heading, she had written:

Men are

- Free
- Strong
- Straight forward/direct
- Easygoing
- Passionate

- Fun/young at heart
- Live in the now

Women are:

- Needy
- Spineless
- Manipulative/controlling
- Bossy
- Irrational
- Dwell in the past
- Nurturing

Laura discussed how she had admired her father, while she had little respect for her mother. She could identify clearly with the above dynamics in her parents' relationship. To Laura her dad had been the fun guy, suffering in a marriage to a woman who could not match his strength or humour. The opposites are obvious:

• Free (ability to be self)	Needy (can't be self need another) also manipulative – not allowing another to be free to act as desired
• Strong	Spineless
• Straight forward/direct	Irrational (going off at tangents as opposed to direct)
• Easygoing	Controlling
• Passionate (expressive)	Unable to express self
• Fun/young at heart (child playful)	Bossy (assuming parent role)
• Living in the now	Living in the past
• Nurtures self	Only can nurture others

When this related to Laura herself, it was clear that her feminine side was being expressed more in Shadow ways which she had attempted to suppress, for fear of becoming like her mother. So strong was her identification with her father, and so rejecting was she of her mother (their current relationship was strained), that she had opted for a gay lifestyle, where she could seek to emulate her father, rather than become her needy, manipulative mother.

Projecting this into her relationships, Laura could now understand why she had been attracted to women just like her mother and why after the initial attraction, their neediness terrified and repelled her, resulting in an inability to remain in long term relationships. Each time she kept facing her mother. To heal Laura would then need to learn to accept those aspects of herself in her Shadow, which related to her view of women.

Here is another example from Ralph:
Men are:

• Strong
• The breadwinners
• Selfish
• Good company in bars etc
• Leaders
• Implement discipline
• Fighters

Women are:

• Soft
• Homemakers
• Kind
• Supportive
• Not sure what else to write

In relating what he had written to his parents' relationship, Ralph could see how much his father had been the overbearing presence in the house, leaving little room for his mother to develop her own sense of self. It had all been about Dad. Consequently, he had identified with his father and realised through this process how little he really knew or understood his mother. She had become this kind, idealised view of a woman with no real understanding of her as a person with hopes, desires and ideals. It was interesting that he found so little to write about when it came to women, a further indication of just how out of balance his own inner male/female is.

He could acknowledge that he had completely suppressed his own femine side, in his desire to be like his father. Women were nonentities, designed to be passive present and little more.

When we shifted this perspective to his married life, Ralph saw with shock that this was true of the woman he had married. He had never really considered that she might have dreams and ambitions that weren't his own. He could also see that in raising his two daughters, he had raised them in many respects as sons. His pride and joy was his older daughter who was an advocate. Seeing his list of male attributes, it was easy to see that she had adopted these, while rejecting those relating to her mother.

Here are Ralph's opposites:

| • Strong | Soft |
| • The breadwinners | Homemakers – belief that they can't support themselves |

- Selfish
- Good company in bars (outside world) etc
- Leaders
- Implement discipline
- Fighters

Kind (giving/generous)
Homemakers i.e. should be at home
Supportive – be led
Kind (weak)
Kind (weak)

In the case of Sue, there are more common wounds than wounds at the opposite end of the same scales. Sue listed the following:

Men are:

- Violent
- Frustrated
- Useless
- Complaining
- Let you down

Women are:

- Jealous
- Don't listen to me
- Have minimal time for fun and enjoyment
- Find nurturing a mission
- Busy

It was easy to see from her lists why Sue was not a happy person: - both her male and female aspects were extremely negative. Parents who were mutually abusive had set the tone for her future relationships and it was not hard to see why she had yet to find a man who she could remain in a relationship with for any length of time.

Looking at the likes and opposites the aspects that emerged most strongly was that women don't listen, and that men are so busy complaining about their own problems, that there is no time to listen and hear about yours. It's clear then that as a child, Sue had never felt heard. One can also see that while men are "useless", and clearly don't work hard, women are the opposite and are working so hard they never can relax and have fun.

Both men and women share the commonality in Sue's world of not being able to nurture – men because they "let you down," and women because there is so much work to get done. Once again it's clear that Sue's parents did not have time to adequately nurture themselves or her.

Jealousy is a sign of insecurity in a relationship. Violence is another sign of insecurity, it's a fiery way of showing insecurity. The hostile withdrawal that frequently accompanies jealousy, is a watery way of demonstrating the same wound.

To bring these two warring factions within herself together, would require much therapeutic work, if Sue was to have any chance of a relationship that surpassed that of her parents'. Fortunately Sue had recognised this and was taking steps to heal herself.

Family Constellation work

In family constellations, as in the earlier analogy of the cells, each atom of the cell moves and vibrates according to the cell structure. If you replace one part of the cell, the other parts will step in to compensate, so that the activity of the cell remains constant. In family constellation work, pioneered by German psychotherapist, Bert Hellinger, he examined the imbalance through generations to family structures through various traumas they had experienced, from still-born births to accidental deaths, illness, divorce and any other tragedies that caused the imbalance. By unravelling these histories, and using random workshop participants to fulfil the roles of the various family members, Hellinger and those who teach his method, created a family cell/unit that mirrors the actual family structure. Now here's the interesting part. While placed in these positions, the participants start to feel or receive information or even actual physical sensations, which cause them to act or speak in the manner in which the actual person would have done.

Through this process information from the past which may have been hidden and or subconscious within the main participant, starts to surface and the person for whom the participants are playing the role, can begin to get some understanding of the root cause of their own issues as expressed through past family dynamics. The participant is now empowered and can, from this position of understanding, choose to forgive, release, detach or do whatever feels appropriate to clear this energy, through each of the role players who energetically respond according to the person they are representing.

Balance then can be restored and love and understanding can replace hurt, anger or guilt. This upgrades the entire energetic level of the family and what's amazing is that it can start healing throughout the family – way beyond the actual family member who did the workshop.

Getting back to the cell analogy, it's as if the one part of the cell in healing, creates the stimulus for the rest of the cell to heal itself and in turn the surrounding cells or family units.

Doing one of these workshops myself, I was amazed at how total strangers, when placed in the positions of my various family members started to act and speak as if they were them. It was uncanny how even mannerisms appeared that related to the people whose energetic role they were being entrusted to represent.

What also was explained, is that if a family does not heal, even if you remove the "bad apple" from the group, another family member will slot into the role. Expand that thinking further and if you imagine a society as a cell rather than simply a group of people, attempting to remove criminals from society will only create space for more to fill, whereas rehabilitating those convicted of crimes helps to heal the wound permanently and lessens the criminal component of the cell/society.

Through this work I saw amazing transformations, as hidden relationships and occurrences were revealed and understanding of patterns relating to unhappiness and events were explored and cleared.

What this did reveal as well to me is how the balance in family, society, corporate and cultural/tribal groups is so interdependent. A wound in the past will repeat itself and become part of the energy dynamic of the group until it is recognised and healed. It may be absent male figures, fear of loss of the females one loves, inability to nurture one's children appropriately, or any other wound, but because of the cell dynamics it is imprinted in the family history. Each wound creates a blockage of energy if not processed and released and this in turn "blocks" the flow of loving energy in the family unit and in the individual. This blockage then is expressed in extremes of behaviour.

Genetically we are told that we carry certain inherent weaknesses or predispositions to certain diseases. This is true, but like the skin that sheds but continues to make the scar, even though the skin is totally new, so we know that our cell dynamics alter according to our thoughts. You may have a genetic predisposition to a certain weakness, but whether it will manifest is related to your ability to understand the stress patterns and triggers within yourself, that put your body out of balance, which then creates the imbalance required for that illness to develop.

I experienced this myself when I went for an annual check-up to my doctor. After taking blood and having various tests he found that I had a genetic disposition to high cholesterol. He was most concerned and sent me for a further cholesterol test. The cholesterol was found to be completely normal and within the safe limits. He found this confusing, as every indication genetically was that I should have high cholesterol. Because I am unstressed (well most of the time!) and lead a relatively healthy lifestyle, it had not manifested. What I do know now though is that should this situation change for whatever reason, one of my weak areas or areas most likely to have problems, will be cholesterol.

What is really being passed on through generations is more a pattern of thinking and reacting, than a physical disposition as such. If breast cancer is rife in your family for instance, then you could examine similar ways of nurturing that may run in your family, as breasts have to do with nurturing. Release the way to nurture in this way and you lessen the chances of following in the family disease.

Bruce Lipton Phd, in his book *The Biology of Belief*, describes an experiment with two rats, both of whom have a genetic disease, making them prone to high blood pressure, diabetes, obesity and a discolouration of the fur. He takes one rat and puts it on a poor diet in a stressful situation, while the other lucky rat gets given a premium diet and a pretty good home setup. What happens is the rat with the poor diet and stressful lifestyle, develops the disease, while the other remains, healthy, lean and disease free.

If we then can live according to rat number two, we lessen the risk of getting ill even if we are genetically disposed to certain illnesses. Identifying what makes us stressed and releasing those issues so that we are in balance and relatively unstressed, is the best way to ensure better health. Bringing ourselves into balance by understanding both ends of the see-saw we swing up and down on, means to do just this.

The more out of balance we are the more our proverbial see-saw will swing, meaning that we will feel more out of sorts, manifest more havoc in our lives and feel less ok with who we are.

Through this previous exercise you have come to understand some of the dynamics within your parents and how they have become part of who you are, both the aspects you perceive as good and those that may be less pleasant. Now we will look at how you used to go about trying to balance yourself and why it may not have worked.

Let me give you an example.

Joe came to see me concerned about his life in general. He is a geologist and as a result of his profession, has had to travel and work abroad for his entire married life. To maintain some stability, his wife has opted to remain in the same city to raise their children.

A subsequent chat with his 20 year old son Thomas revealed that the young man felt resentful towards his father for his long absences and consequential lack of involvement with the boy's life.

Thomas has chosen to enter the navy. It is not hard to understand why. The young man felt a deep hurt at not having a father who was there for him in his youth and as a result he was drawn to the navy, which provided a whole battalion of father figures to make up for his childhood.

What Thomas was not aware of was that through this choice, he was repeating an ancestral pattern. If he married, which he intended to do, as a sailor, it would mean that he would most likely have to spend long periods away from his home, wife and family, as is the situation for most men and women in the forces.

Back to Joe and a bit of probing which revealed that his father had been a high powered business man, with a result that he had spent much time travelling. When he was at home he was preoccupied, distant emotionally and found it hard to communicate with his family particularly Joe. Joe had always believed that he had never quite matched up to his father's expectations of him.

Going back into the family history, it was revealed that Joe's grandfather, a pilot in the First World War, had been shot down and killed, when Joe's father was only three. He had grown up then with a very dominating mother figure and an absence of a father figure.

Can you see the pattern that weaves itself throughout the generations?
– a lack of a father figure, physically and/or emotionally.

- Joe's grandfather = absent physically and emotionally from Joe's father due to early death in the army
- Joe's father = absent physically and emotionally from Joe due to career selection and an inability to deal with his emotional upheaval due to his own war trauma experiences
- Joe = absent physically and emotionally from Thomas due to career selection
- Thomas in the navy = absent physically and emotionally for his future family

If Joe had not come for help, this same pattern may have continued throughout the following generations. As it is, there is a chance that if Joe heals his own wounds brought about through his father's emotional absence; he may be able to help his own son heal and release some of his hurt, masquerading as anger. This benefit will then be passed on to Thomas's future family.

Like the scar on our skin, the original wounding many generations ago may long be past but it keeps re-appearing with each generation. It is as if the family cell has programmed itself this way.

Chapter Seven

Four types of relationships

---

1. The Independent relationship

He likes to have holidays skiing in Austria, she prefers relaxing on a tropical beach. He likes kite boarding, she prefers the gym. He seldom goes out, but prefers to play computer games. She is always socialising with friends. He works long hours and so does she – in different offices and often continents. Now there is no harm in having different interests, in fact it's healthy in a relationship, but when the interests become so diversified and consuming that the relationship drifts further apart with little or no emotional connection, that's an independent relationship.

The first relationship involves two people that are completely separate. Each person in the relationship is completely estranged from the other. They may feel alone, unsupported by their partner, misunderstood and may question why they are in the relationship that seems to offer them little in return.

The term "independent relationship," is in itself a misnomer, because by definition, a relationship is defined as a connection by persons between blood or marriage, or an association or involvement, while the term 'independent' means to not be influenced or controlled by others or to act alone. From this one understands then that an independent relationship is not a relationship at all. There is no communication other than superficial daily needs, no intimacy and while their may be mutual respect, the relationship is so polarised as to be defined by two strangers sharing an abode.

This type of relationship seldom lasts long term, simply because it is in our nature to crave intimacy and when this need is not being met and there is no need to be with the other in order to survive, such as in the case of a co-dependent relationship, then one or both of the partners will in time move on.

2. The co-dependent relationship.

In a co-dependent relationship the couple may not even like each other, but each party is bound to the other through fear and possibly guilt. The image shows two people completely enmeshed in each other to the extent of losing their own identities.

How do you identify this type of relationship, which is the most common of all three types of relationships?

The following list may help you:

1. **Denial** – denying that there is anything wrong with the relationship. Many times I have counselled one partner who is desperately unhappy in the relationship, only to have the other party deny that anything is wrong at all. If you probe further, they may gloss over the fact that they have days without speaking, where one party is sulking, they may allude to the lack of sex but may find a justifiable reason for that and may even joke about the situation, anything but admit that there is a problem.

2. **Guilt** coupled with shame is often present, leading to self hatred and a low sense of self esteem.

3. **Feeling victimised.** Each partner will portray their day at work/lot in life/contribution to the other etc as being harder/less appreciated/less supported etc. When the partner does not show adequate sympathy or "support," they can become hurt, resentful and even angry.

4. **No growth.** When the relationship is not one of growth, but rather of apathy and stagnation and even degeneration in terms of ones' sense of self.

5. **Control and manipulation.** With neither party feeling empowered, situations have to be either manipulated (*deflated* from a lack of self worth) or controlled (*inflated* from a need to boost lack of self worth). With the use of control, fear often plays a part. In that if I don't do what you want me to, I will make you angry, cause you to leave, cause you to stop giving me money etc. You may do things for the other under the guise of kindness, whereas in reality it's a form of control.

6. **Problems in confronting situations.** Either by avoidance or angry outbursts. Once again the polar opposites apply, but the wound of being unable to appropriately deal with conflict still applies. Women, more often than men, believe that to express their anger is "not nice". That their partner will leave if they do so. The situation boils in suppressed resentment until something (very often something unrelated and small) sparks it off and a tirade happens. In some relationships the matter is never dealt with and it may simmer for years, or one partner or both may withdraw and sulk or not communicate for days in a display of passive aggressive behaviour.

7. **Smothering.** The belief that somehow being in a relationship should involve sacrificing all ones own needs and desires for the sake of the other. To become one with the partner involves losing all sense of self. A kind of enmeshment in which there is only room for one person, the other must dissolve their identity in order to be with the other. Some people might believe that to do anything without the other is tantamount to saying "I don't love or need you."

8. **Criticism.** One party or both continually criticises the other. Whether it's the cooking, bringing up the children, how they spend their free-time or any other activity, its most often met with disapproval and the feeling that you have somehow failed.

9. **Lack of trust.** Often there may be issues of trust. One partner or both may feel insecure and this may result in not trusting the other or their may be past infidelities, resulting in a lack of trust. This can prove to be stifling to the other partner if they are constantly checked upon.

10. There are **huge expectations** placed on each other, such as "I believe it is your job to make me happy." "I expect you to support me," "you should be the strong one," "I expect you to do all the housework," "you should understand my feelings, even if I don't express or verbalise them," and so on. When these expectations are not met, the other party feels let down and resentful. There is a shift of responsibility so that in order for me to be content and fulfilled/happy you must do what I expect you should do, i.e. my happiness is your responsibility. When you don't do or act in a way I feel you should do, I will make you feel guilty and ashamed. This projection of shame and guilt causes the partner's self-esteem to spiral downwards and makes both partners feel like victims of their circumstances. The guilt also then makes us believe that to redeem ourselves means to accept inappropriate behaviour or sacrifice our own dreams and desires.

11. **Using sex as a tool for punishment** (withholding sex) or reward (when they have done what you manipulated them to do. An example would be when a woman was refusing to have sex with her husband. The day he arrived home with a new car for her however, she allowed him to do so.

12. There is a **belief in scarcity rather than abundance,** and this affects all aspects of life, from financial to love. The belief is that there is not enough to go around or that what is there, will be depleted or taken away. Love and money are intertwined and measured. There may be separate bank accounts where each penny spent is accounted for and owed to one by the other. If money = energy, then one may give, conditionally and expect reimbursement in some form.

13. **Lack of intimacy** and fully loving and accepting the other for who they are.

14. **No real communication of feelings.** There may be a belief that it's not appropriate to talk about one's problems or feelings – that in some way its more heroic and strong to remain silent or doing so might result in the other partner believing they are under attack.

15. **Perfectionism.** The expectation is that the other must behave perfectly, must do everything the "right" way (according to the other partner's view

of what is right. Even if the one party behaves badly such as getting drunk, driving dangerously, flirting, screaming abuse etc, the belief is that the other partner should not behave this way – a case of do as I say, not as I do and don't question my actions even though I am free to do so to you. When confronted with this discrepancy, denial or anger usually result.

16. **Giving and receiving are out of balance,** with each partner feeling that they do the bulk of the giving for which they feel they receive little. A man may feel he does all the giving by providing financially, while the woman may feel that she does the most giving, by providing a tidy home, child care and meals. Both believe their contribution is greater. The reason for your doing so much though is more to make them need you rather than out of pure kindness. In doing so you enable them to rely on you, which puts you in a position of control.

17. **Lying between parties** occurs regularly. If there is no truth, then there can be no intimacy. The fear of truth is what stops us from being intimate.

18. **The need to rescue the other party**, which is often confused with loving them. This is reason why you may find the co-dependent person marries a string of people who all have similar issues. You probably know at least one person who married an alcoholic only to divorce them and marry another person with a substance dependency problem.

19. **Fear of being abandoned** by the other, because each partner deep down, does not feel good about who they are and believes that they are not worthy of a loving relationship. This may even result in deliberately sabotaging the relationship as a way of trying to feel in control – "let me do it before they do it" thinking.

20. **Substance abuse.** An emptiness that each may try to fill with alcohol, drugs, smoking, work, infidelities, shopping sprees or eating disorders.

21. **Feeling responsible for the other person's actions.** One person in the relationship may have an exaggerated sense of responsibility for the other's actions. "I get so embarrassed when John embellishes his stories/has no manners/drinks too much/swears etc in company, that I don't want to go out with him."

22. **Boundary issues.** Either rigid boundaries or no boundaries at all. In such relationships letters to the other or emails may be read without consent, telephone messages "spied" upon. There may be rigid controls in terms of where one partner can go and with whom etc. This relates back to point No. nine, about trust.

23. **Difficulty in viewing yourself as a separate person,** with your own desires, needs and aspirations. You become meshed in the other person's life

to the exclusion of your own and may often not even know what it is you want from life, save possibly that your partner change.

24. **Frustrated creativity** – neither feeling able to express their creativity in the form they would like to and blaming others for not being able to do so, such as "if I didn't have to work/clean/cook/look after the children etc then I could do what I want to do."

You may have identified with a number of points listed and it would not be surprising, as this is by far the most common form of relationship. In the past, the term co-dependency was linked more exclusively to relationships where substance abuse, such as alcoholism and drug addiction were a problem. However, more commonly now, it encompasses a pattern of dysfunctional behaviour in relationships and the families affected by their behaviour.

It must also be understood, that there are degrees of co-dependency and that the majority of relationships will at some time display some aspects listed above, but may not be categorised as "co-dependent." Most of us though will, to greater or lesser extent show signs of co-dependency. Why? Simply because few of us are whole, and by that I mean balanced and integrated with both our male and female aspects. Because we are not, we will project this on the world outside ourselves, creating relationships that are not in balance. There is no black and white as to when a relationship becomes co-dependent and when it is not, rather there are degrees or a grey scale of co-dependency.

Usually, the one partner is more controlling, needy and emotionally withdrawn, characteristics that the other person then attempts to make compensation for, at the expense of their own needs and desires. Obviously this cannot provide for a balanced and fulfilling relationship.

In extreme cases, in an attempt to ensure that the "pleasing party" remains in the relationship, the "ruling party" may resort to abusive behaviour in order that the "pleasing party" doesn't walk out on them. By being abusive and eating away at the self-worth of the "pleasing party," they attempt to ensure that the "pleasing party" believes that they actually deserve this treatment and that it is in some way their fault.

What is this really all about?

A co-dependent relationship is a relationship that is out of balance. One person gives too much, the other takes too much etc: Look at the list below of opposites often found in this type of relationship:

Does too much	Does too little*
Gives too much	Gives too little
Overtly responsible	Shirks responsibility

Blames self	Blames others
Rescues	Needy i.e. needs rescuing
Need for recognition/approval	Withholds recognition as a way to control
Difficulty/guilt with expressing anger	Angry outbursts directed at others
Need to manipulate	Need to control
Lack of trust in self	Lack of trust in others
Fear of rejection	Fear of being alone
No boundaries	Invasive boundaries
Problems making decisions	Make decisions on self needs
Difficulty identifying feelings	Difficulty expressing feelings (except anger)
Rescuer	Victim
Accepting	Belittling/abusive

* Note: Often one person will do too little because whenever they do try to do something, their attempts may be criticised as their partner's martyr archetype becomes threatened. You can't be a martyr while your partner is helping, so to maintain the illusion of how wrong your partner is, you criticise what he or she does, so you have to do it all yourself. In some relationships though, one person may simply be idle.

Exercise:

Here are some questions that you can answer to determine the degree to which you may be in a co-dependent relationship. Tick which questions apply to you.

1. Are you unhappy and unfulfilled in your relationship?
2. Do you want to change things about your partner's behaviour?
3. Do you often feel resentful towards your partner?
4. Do you feel that you give too much in the relationship and keep very little time, money etc for yourself?
5. Do you struggle to meet the approval of others and does it concern you when you don't have their approval?
6. Do you often sacrifice your own needs and desires in order to try to win their approval?
7. Are you afraid to voice your anger and rather steer clear of an argument?
8. Would it be correct to say that your relationship breaks you down more than builds you up?
9. If your partner goes off and follows a sporting interest, study interest or social activity without you, do you feel hurt and offended?
10. Do you sometimes question your value?
11. Do you desire yet fear intimacy?

12. Do you feel a lot of pressure to be perfect or do things correctly?
13. Is it hard for you to receive compliments and some times even gifts because you find giving easier than receiving?
14. Is it hard for you to ask for help?
15. Is saying "no" difficult for you?
16. Do you feel that no one really likes you or that you have a low sense of self- esteem?
17. Is it hard for you to tell people how you really feel?
18. Are you unsure of what you want to do with your life and yet are not happy with the state it's in?
19. Do you feel that without your input in the family, things would go to pieces?
20. Do you start things but seldom finish them?
21. Do you feel uncomfortable unless you are doing something? i.e. doing nothing equates to being of no worth?
22. Do you often feel as if you are helping others and yet no-one is there for you?
23. Do you often feel guilty or to blame for situations that have occurred?

If you answered yes to many of those questions, then the chances are that you are in a relationship that is not in balance. If unsure perhaps you should seek the advice of a trained therapist to help you with these issues. There is no black and white area when a relationship is co-dependent as already mentioned – just degrees of co-dependency. So answering yes to arguably five questions would mean you still have a pretty healthy relationship. When you start to go over 10 you are heading into the area where you need to be aware or working to improve your relationship. Over fifteen and it may be time to seek help to change things and improve your happiness and fulfilment.

This is a story of a relationship that was an extreme version of a co-dependent relationship. Jill had been married to an alcoholic and when the problem became irredeemable (he was not prepared to get the help he needed,) the marriage ended.

A few years later, Jill met a man who seemed the opposite of her troubled first husband. He was a respected lawyer, a devoutly religious man by all accounts, and appeared loving and in love with her. Consequently she agreed to marry him. Over the 15 years of their marriage, things went steadily downhill, as he too, took to wild bouts of drinking often followed by violent and abusive outbursts. By now they had two children and leaving him, from a financial perspective, was not an option , she felt. The drinking continued, in spite of his work. Drinking sessions were intermingled with spending sprees which put pressure on their budget. Jill started working as his bookkeeper to try to keep tabs on the practise and him. She was terrified that he may make a fool of himself in court or make a decision that would cost his reputation. He still denied any problem and often would appear not to drink at social events, while doing so on the sly. The children started picking up on their father's behaviour and mirroring his abuse to Jill. His drinking was becoming more apparent to those around him including his colleagues. Jill rescued him by apologising, blaming his behaviour to colleagues on pressure and generally tidying up after the emotional and financial mess he left trailing behind him. In trying to please him and avoid another outburst, she avoided meeting her own needs and gave non-stop to him and the family. In the numbness she created to protect herself emotionally, she also became numb to her own feelings and would dismiss his behaviour lightly, as some sort of funny little idiosyncrasy.

After another unpleasant tirade where he was yelling abusively at her and his children, her response was typical of a co-dependent: "Oh well, I guess every family has its problems - he'll be fine tomorrow." In this there was total denial of the problem and the impact it was having on her and the family.

3. The interdependent relationship

When we ourselves are in balance, we allow for the interdependent relationship. This is the relationship where each person is responsible for his or her own needs and does not hold the other accountable for their happiness or lack of it.

It is where two people walk side by side and are there to share intimacy and assist each other, without demanding or expecting the other to be or act in a certain way.

This is where each person feels fulfilled and realises that through the relationship both parties are growing and assisting each other. The whole then is greater than the parts. Intimacy and sharing of emotions happens freely and there is a deep rooted trust between both parties. Their joy is your joy and their happiness is not threatening to you, but a blessing.

As two separate beings, each individual meets and shares intimacy with the other without losing all sense of self. Just as I listed points that are often common in a co-dependent relationship, here are some points prevalent in an interdependent relationship.

1. **A willingness to confront** and work with aspects of the relationship that either party feel may not be working.
2. **An absence of guilt and blame** and no attempt to impose either on the other party.
3. **Healthy sense of self esteem** as opposed to the over or under inflated ego which is the mark of low self esteem. An acceptance of your own character and its possible defects which, unlike a co-dependent relationship, you don't attempt to project on the other.
4. **Owning responsibility for one's life.** A shift from victim mentality to where each party owns responsibility for their lives and the situations that occur within those lives.
5. **The relationship stimulates and expands each person**'s sense of self and life experience.
6. **No desire or need to control or manipulate** the other person.
7. **An ability to truly convey one's feelings** without blame or guilt. Communication is open and there is no hidden resentment etc. Each person is able to be self-assertive and knows that even if they do say something the other may not like, their partner will attempt to listen and see the situation through their partners eyes as well as their own.
8. **Trust.** Each party trusts the other implicitly and is honest with the other.
9. **Encouragement.** Each party will do whatever they can to encourage the other to achieve their goals and desires and feel joyous in that achievement, even if it requires separation at times.
10. **No expectations.** As one man said, "I try each day to start on a new page and not hold onto past experiences, so that I don't project them onto the way I expect my partner to behave today."

11. **An acceptance of all that is, as being perfect for what you need to experience.**
12. **A belief in abundance.** There is abundant love, energy, money etc in the universe.
13. **No need to be right.** The understanding that what may feel right for you may not be so for your partner and imposing your right way on them is inappropriate. There is no one right way.
14. **Balanced giving and receiving** according to the shifting daily needs of the relationship. The acceptance that some days you may do more because your partner is otherwise occupied and trusting that the situation will balance.
15. **An easiness between both partners to shift between male and female roles**. One day it may be necessary for a man to make lunch for the kids, while she may need to mow the lawn on another day and both partners are okay with this. You can shift between so called male duties and female duties with ease and are not terrified to step out of these limitations.
16. **True love and unconditional acceptance of the other** without criticism or judgement. An ability to share feelings, knowing they won't be criticised or judged.
17. **Supportive of the other without doing it for them.** This may mean that some times you have to stand back and let each other explore a path, even if it doesn't feel right for you. I recall when my husband joined a cult, mistakenly believing that this was a genuine path to mysticism and enlightenment. Every bone in my body said it was not what it reported to be, however, I knew that if I blocked his way he would resent me for it. I needed to stand back and let him experience his journey and, when it did emerge to be a cult, be there to help him work through his anger and hurt, without saying: "I told you so" and realising that he would do the same for me.
18. **You are each fulfilled,** in your integrity and inspire each other to be the very best you can be. As such you can truly be yourself at all times. You are both centred and balanced between your archetypes. You realise that in truth you cannot and should not be responsible for any other person (with the exception of young children) other than yourself.
19. You have complete **respect** for each others boundaries.
20. **You see yourself and your partner as separate people,** each with your own needs, aspirations and goals, which you respect, honour and encourage and don't feel threatened by their success. You are each aware of your own needs and feelings and respect those of each other.

21. There is **flexibility** in the relationship as opposed to rigidity.
22. **Creativity** forms an integral part of both your lives, be it in a traditional artistic manner, or expressed through cooking, creating companies, gardening, writing etc.

In this type of relationship, you are not together simply to survive, but to thrive. You each add to the other's life. Now for most people weighed down by a relationship that is co-dependent, the above list may seem to be some kind of fantasy. The truth is we can have this type of relationship, but we have to be prepared to change and that's the hard part.

When I worked as a telephone counsellor the words I most frequently ran into were: Yes, but…" "Yes, but its not a good time now," "Yes, but, he wouldn't agree," "Yes, but, I can't afford to." And so on. The minute we have to change is when all our resistances build up a large wall, which we express through "yes, but." If you find yourself saying those words, look to where it is that you are resisting change and ask yourself why. That's why, if we don't change and wait hoping our partner will, the result is naturally a stalemate, where nothing happens (except more resentment).

How do we move from co-dependency or independent relationships to interdependent relationships?

1. Recognising where we are not in balance, is the first step.
2. The second step is owning the imbalance as opposed to making it someone else's fault or responsibility, such as "my bad childhood, my mother's behaviour, my father's absence, his selfishness, her lack of support" and so on. (Acknowledging these is fine, making them the reason to remain stuck there is not.)
3. The third step is bringing ourselves into balance, so that we attract a similar partner. From this point of being we get together with another person not out of the need to use them to make ourselves feel whole, but rather because we recognise that to be in a relationship, is to challenge ourselves to grow and develop even more. As such, when we find ourselves not in a relationship, we don't fall apart and choose appropriate partners rather than be alone, we are content with the wholeness of our own being and should a partner appear then it would enhance what we already have as opposed to fill a gap in what we feel we haven't got.
4. Give up wanting revenge on a partner. Forgiveness itself is not required when we come to see that we needed the person to behave in a way to balance ourselves. In reality they played the role required, so in essence there is nothing to forgive. Your partner is only the messenger. Don't shoot him/her!

4. Dependent Relationships

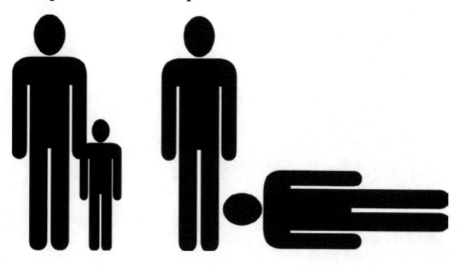

There is a fourth type of relationship, which is identified as **dependent** relationship. This is when one party is completely dependent on the other, such as a child, an invalid or an elderly impoverished parent. The relationship is usually relatively short as a person heals or passes on, or as a child grows. The relationship then alters to one of the other relationships described above.

Your relationship: In growth or decline?

Because nothing in the universe is ever static, it is always in a process of growth or decay. If your relationship is not growing or improving, then inevitably it will be getting worse. Like anything else in life, relationships take work. You have the power, no matter how impossible it seems, to reverse the process of degeneration. In the beginning you both may have been prepared to do anything for each other, now that may have changed. You will need to re-engage with that willingness to work, if you want to create a better relationship with yourself and as a result, with your partner, or you may decide to start a new relationship if the situation feels hopeless.

Remember though, that if relationships are projections of our own issues, until you work with these, you will merely carry them with you into the next relationship, which is why we can see so often in hindsight that we have repeated our mistakes. Consequently working with yourself before embarking on a new relationship may ensure a better result. As the saying goes, banging your head repeatedly against a wall is not necessarily mad. Doing so and expecting a different result each time is!

Chapter Eight

The Child and the Parent

Opposites that attract

There are thousands of different archetypes, some more "popular," than others. In this section of the book, I have listed some common archetypes and their opposites, to help you identify which ones are at play in your relationship.

It's important to note that we all have a number of different archetypes that come to the fore depending on the circumstances, relationship etc. So I would expect that you would be able to see yourself mirrored in a number of the examples given. Perhaps the most common of all is:

"David, have you done the washing up yet?"

He sighs, ignores her and continues fiddling with the TV remote control and watching TV.

"David, it's your night to do the dishes. You never do what I ask you to."

"Give me a break, I've had a shockingly bad day" is his reply, or he may just pretend he hasn't heard her.

This conversation may seem fairly typical if it were between a child and parent, but for many people, this interaction would typify the communication between two adults. This is when the relationship is made up of the opposites of the Parent and the Child.

In the old days of apartheid in South Africa, one of the Prime Ministers, PW Botha, had the habit of wagging his finger at his audience. Whenever he appeared on TV or in public addressing his supporters, out came the pointing finger.

What did this indicate about the role he was playing?

He positioned himself as the critical Parent, judging his subjects who he clearly viewed as errant children. Much of apartheid saw this unhealthy Parent/Child role being played out, particularly when it came to the black population. The government at the height of apartheid rule, did treat the non-white population as children, in that they were not allowed out after certain hours, they could not drink alcohol, they had to carry passes at all times and could not marry across the racial barrier ("big daddy" said who you could and couldn't marry).

Perhaps the most common of all is the Child and the Parent. Even in one to one relationships, this Parental/Child imbalance was played out, to the point of calling a gardener "boy," when he could be older than his employee, or a domestic helper, a "girl." These servants were then taken care of (to a greater or lesser degree,) by the "baas," (the Afrikaans word for "boss"). Labourers on farms, often received rations in lieu of payment or as part payment, as they were considered too irresponsible (child-like) to manage their affairs without Adult supervision. This relationship between a leader and his subjects represented the very worst in the archetypal roles of Parent and Child. Understandably, the "Children" in this relationship went from withdrawing in passive aggressive resentment, to rebelling against their white "Parents."

A relationship between two adults, that plays itself out in the archetypes of a Child and Parent, is unlikely to be a fulfilling one. If we are an adult, then ideally we need to relate to each other as adults. Sometimes in moments of spontaneous play, both being in a child archetype may be fun, while when one partner is ill and in need of care, a nurturing parental role from the other partner may be appropriate. However, on a day to day basis, most of us desire to be in an adult to adult relationship.

In 1964, Eric Berne an MD who had studied psychiatry wrote a book entitled: *Games People Play*, where he wrote about Transactional Analysis. The core concept of Transactional Analysis, as I understand it, is that there are three potential roles we can play, namely: Parent, Adult and Child. Each of these archetypal roles (with the exception of the Adult), has two aspects to them which are either functional or dysfunctional. (Berne indicated the state of being from the actual child, adult or parent, by using capital letters, which I have done to indicate all archetypal roles in this book.)

The Parent can be:
Positive:

1. Nurturing and encouraging
2. Controlling in a structural manner, such as setting boundaries

Negative

1. Spoiling
2. Critical, domineering and controlling

The Adult: Objective, logical and rational

The Child can be either:
Positive:

1. The child can either be present as natural, playful and free or
2. Co-operative and helpful with others

Negative:

1. Fearful, resistant or rebellious
2. Immature

Identifying the Parent and Child

Behaviour

Only seven percent of our communication is verbal. According to Albert Mehrabian, Professor Emeritus of Psychology, UCLA. the main way we communicate is via facial expression (55%) and the remaining 38% by the way we say the words[1]. Non verbal facial expressions include:

1. Rolling your eyes
2. Shrugging your shoulders
3. Giggling
4. Substance abuse
5. Pointing or waving your index finger
6. Impatient body language
7. Raising eyebrows
8. Sighing
9. Turning your body away
10. Listening with interest
11. Crossing your arms
12. Body distance
13. Touch
14. Eye contact

Speech:

In relationships, the negative Parent and Child archetypes manifest when one partner assumes the critical, controlling and domineering role, while the other person becomes the negative child, and is resistant, passively aggressive, immature or rebellious. When in these archetypal roles, we speak as if we are the Parent or Child.

Exercise:

Run through this list below and tick the expressions and behaviour you use frequently with your partner. Then let your partner do the same. (If you are unsure, make a copy of the list and keep it handy and each time you say something along the lines of the phrases below mark it off). Add the score after a few days. Then give yourselves a score to see who is playing what role.

1. Any superlatives relating to oneself and designed to impress others, such as I was the fastest, cleverest/slimmest/fittest/best educated etc
2. I'm busy I'll do it later… (and then don't).
3. I deserve to have some fun… when we have behaved unacceptably
4. I don't care
5. Nobody understands me
6. Everyone always mocks me
7. Things never work out right for me
8. I wish
9. I want
10. Calling your partner: Mom, Mummy, Pop, Pa, daddy, etc
11. Don't you dare
12. Under no circumstances
13. Why don't you…
14. You don't know what its like
15. Never…or You never…
16. Patronising language
17. Haven't you learnt yet…? or Haven't you done … yet?
18. Passing negative judgements such as "Now look what you've done," or "You always mess things up" and words such as "stupid, bad, crazy, or ugly," and so on.
19. Do this! Stop doing that!
20. I'm sick of you're not….
21. In my opinion
22. I believe
23. I think
24. I understand: Saying things like: "I understand that you are feeling angry…)" reflecting back the other persons emotions/feelings.
25. How do you feel we can solve the problem?
26. I see
27. I realise
28. Starting sentences with: Why, what, how, when
29. I don't agree with you but I accept that you don't feel the same way I do.
30. I appreciate…..

Create three headings: Child, Adult and Parent. For any ticks next to 1-10 give yourself one point under the heading Child. For any ticks next to 11-20 put one point under Parent and for any ticks next to 21-30, give yourself points under Adult. If you are unsure ask someone else to monitor your speech for a few days. Now examine your behaviour.

It should be easy to see under which category you fall into most often, as your way of interacting with your partner.

In the role of the Parent, we re-enact or mimic the experiences we had with authority figures as Children in the way we speak, behave, feel and think. Foremost would be our parents, but other authority figures, such as teachers, older family members, coaches, scout masters etc would also have played a role. It's how we were taught through experience that adults should act. If our parents shouted when angry with us, then when we play the role of parent in a relationship with a partner, we'll do the same. If they were highly critical of our choices or actions, then our critical Parent will act the same way towards the Child.

In the role of the Child, we revert in our speech, behaviour, feeling and thinking to what we did as a child. If our "Parental" partner scolds us, we may feel shame and squirm, or look away, feel helpless and powerless, while repressing our anger, much the same as we did as a child.

It is only through engaging with our adult selves, that we can change our behaviour of the Parent/Child and balance our relationship from that of parent/child to adult/adult. In the role of adult, we can react in present time (not based on past conditioning,) using our ability to think and act for ourselves. To be in ones adult self then is to be integrated and to engage others with interest, with no fear of being threatened or being threatening. Here we are straightforward, there is no game-playing and our reasoning is sound. It is here that we experience ourselves as empowered and fulfilled.

While there are relationships that last for many years based on the Child/Parent roles, they are seldom fulfilling, yet clearly each person does benefit from assuming that role or else, presumably they would not remain in the relationship. For the Child it could be feeling "safe" with Mummy/Daddy and never having to take real responsibility for anything, while for the Parent it may provide the benefit of feeling in charge and in control. Take this into the bedroom however, and as no-one would really want to make love to a Child or a Parent, so sex is seldom really an intimate and long-term enjoyable experience for either party, particularly if the Child is the man in the relationship.

Examples of conversations between a Parent and Child may be as follows:

Parent (negative): Haven't you paid this account yet?
Child (negative): Stop nagging me I'll do it when I have the time! I've had a seriously bad day.

The Parent/Child conversation may continue along the lines of:

Parent: I can never trust you to do anything. I always end up having to do everything around here!
Child: You're always going on at me! (Followed by withdrawing into hostile silence, and passively aggressively rebelling by not paying the account.)

If the Child realised the game that was being played they may consciously switch into their Adult along the lines of:

Parent: (negative) Haven't you paid this account yet?
Adult: No, just leave it on my desk and I'll pay it this afternoon.

In doing this, the Child has brought the situation into balance, as the Parent cannot act the parental role if there is no Child.

The same situation between two Adults would go something along these lines:

Adult: Have you paid this account yet?
Adult: No, just leave it on my desk and I'll pay it this afternoon.

Another example might be:

Parent: You don't know what it's like having to do a job I loathe, simply to feed the family, while you relax at home.
Child: You don't even begin to try to understand what it's like looking after two toddlers all on my own. At least you are mixing with adults in the workplace. I feel alone and like some giant dishwasher. I wish I could run away from this life.

What's happening here is that both parties are attempting to out victimise their situation.

If the Parent were to connect with their adult self then rationality, understanding and logic would occur, such as:

Parent become Adult: Yes, I can understand that it must get lonely and I can see that being an intelligent woman, it is natural that you would feel frustration having little intellectual stimulation. But we all really do appreciate just how much you do and in the long run what you are doing with the kids in being with them, is amazing.
Child becomes Adult: Wow, thanks for seeing that. I sometimes don't think in your busy life you do appreciate what I do so it's nice to hear. Perhaps as far as you are concerned, its time to start looking at what your career alternatives might be even it it means my getting some part-time work to help out in the transition period..

Can you see the difference in where this Adult to Adult conversation is heading as opposed to if they had remained in their Parent/Child roles?

Sometimes these roles get reversed between actual parents and children, where the child starts talking to the adult as if they were a child. In work situations, the manager may treat his employees as children and assume the parental controlling and domineering role. The employees will then rebel by doing the minimal amount of work, attempting to please in a childlike manner, or passively aggressively start rebelling by sabotaging their superior whenever possible. Even nicking the Postits and other stationary, can be a way of resisting being treated like a child. If a manager is a critical Parent, his staff will, because of the nature of balance, be forced to respond as children. Any verbal or visible rebelling will see the employee labelled as inciting trouble and he or she may end up being fired, in order for the Parental boss to remain in control. What happens in time then, is a company of Yes-men who think, act and behave as children, which will negatively impact on the growth and effectiveness of the company.

I worked with one woman who would use her Child when confronted by an irate superior (see Parent). Her way of responding was to revert to coquettish behaviour with her eyes cast down and talking in a childlike manner. Sometimes this would go as far as her electing to sit on the male employers' laps, in an attempt to win them over via childlike flirtatious behaviour. It was clearly the way she had diffused potentially explosive situations as a child and while it did the same in her adult life; it did not win the respect (or promotional prospects) of her superiors, for whom she would remain a "cute kid."

With her own children, she slid to the opposite end of the see-saw and became the critical Parent. Yelling at them, hitting then and criticising whatever they did constantly, to the point that they withdrew and her behaviour *appeared* to have no effect on them..

When we are playing the role of critical Parent we will live in frustration – no-one wants to be in a relationship with a Child, long term. Part of our criticism may follow along the lines of "won't you grow up!" One woman had a husband who would always play the role of the irresponsible, drunken fun-man at parties. People came to expect him to be the life and soul socially. His actions meant that she went into the role of critical, disapproving Parent to balance his actions, which left him feeling remorseful and apologetic the following day and her angry and resentful. With this dynamic, sex fell away, resulting in him withdrawing into a childlike display of withheld anger.

A divorced man, married again to a woman ten years younger than himself. The honeymoon was short lived when she saw a side of him she had not seen before the marriage. She had joined with him to form a business and things were not going well. Not only did she find herself responsible for the financial well-being of the business, but when he took to being rude and throwing temper tantrums with their clients, family and friends, she found herself in the role of peacemaker, having to step in, pick up the pieces, make excuses and generally cover for him. Likewise when he went on drinking binges, she had to sort out any issues caused as a result of his behaviour. She soon adopted the role of disapproving Parent and he assumed the role of the rebellious Child. The more of a Child he felt the more he was angry and rebelled and the more critical of his behaviour she became.

When playing the role of the fearful or rebellious Child, we may fear our Parent, but be angry with them at the same time. Obviously this will block intimacy and fulfilment in the relationship.

Often we use language to convey the dynamic of a relationship. Think about terms like "babe," "baby," "doll," "chick," all of which reduce a woman to being a Child, which the Parent, in this case a man, can dominate.

Finding balance - How we can change from one archetype to its opposite

Paul owned his own company in which he employed 12 women and a man. He treated his staff with care to the point that he viewed them almost as family. As such he was lenient with their failings and work ethics and would rather work late himself than inconvenience any of them. He did however feel powerful in controlling his "harem." He could be seen to have assumed the role of the nurturing Parent, while his staff lazed in the security of their childlike roles.

The payback was easy to identify.

The staff had the security of a non-taxing and well paid job, while he felt empowered having such a loyal and easily malleable staff. At the office he was admired and constantly asked for his opinion and decisions. It wasn't great for the company though, as no one really wanted to assume responsibility when James was not around and an excess of staff meant he was not utilizing his resources and the company paid for it with a diminished profit. He knew this was happening, but did not want to rock the boat for fear of upsetting his "little family."

At home however it was a different story. Here James felt like the Child, while his wife assumed the role of the disgruntled and disapproving Parent. As he walked through the front door James felt his power diminish. Surrounded by screaming toddlers who seemed unaware of his managerial status and a wife who berated his lack of attempts to help, he found home a most uncomfortable place to be and would happily stay at the office, rather than return home.

This switching of roles between Parent and Child in different circumstances is not uncommon. While with our partners we may be a Parent, we may as easily become a Child at work or vice-versa. If you repeat the quiz above with yourself in a different role, you may see the same reversal apply to yourself as it did to James.

If I had spoken to Paul's wife, I may well have discovered that she herself was an insecure child or a rebellious one in different circumstances.

Not only can these roles swing in different relationships, but they can also do so during the course of the same relationship.

When Tom met Suzanne, he had been in the army for two years, had traveled widely and had had a number of girlfriends. He automatically fell into the role of the Parent with Suzanne who was far less worldly. She, in the role of the Child, became rebellious and immature in the presence of his domination, particularly after a few drinks. She would be loud and generally make a fool of herself to the disapproval of Tom. After such spectacles, he would often threaten to leave her.

This game continued for years until Tom threw up his nine to five job to branch out on his own. Suzanne found herself in the role of the major breadwinner. She also started to show talent in the workplace that saw her move into a position of some power in the company, with the accompanying benefits of company car, secretary etc. While she was climbing the corporate ladder with agility and speed, Tom was struggling to get clients. He became depressed and insecure, refusing to chase up outstanding accounts or likely job prospects. At this point the roles of Parent and Child reversed, and it was Tom who sulked and withdrew in passive aggressive behavior, refusing to do tasks that Suzanne, the Parent had set for him.

Just as we can be both a Parent and a Child dependent on the company we are in, so we can also switch roles within a relationship, depending on outside factors.

The Payoff

"She says I'm her second child," he joked. The man was fifty with boyish good looks and a statement like this was a dead giveaway as to the nature of their relationship. When he referred to his wife later as "mummy," it was very apparent that part of him clearly enjoyed his Peter Pan role. He was the boy who never wanted to grow up. It may be hard to believe why a man would not want to be a man as such, yet there are many perceived advantages to clinging to our roles, otherwise we would not do so.

This man may have enjoyed not having to be responsible for anything in the home. Being responsible at the office was enough. Having a "mother" albeit an occasionally critical one, may have been comforting for him; a chance to opt out and play. Its not fun to have to assume responsibility, to do so means making decisions, which if prove to be wrong later, one has to assume responsibility for:- far easier then to avoid any form of responsibility so that your critical parent can't hold you accountable.

However, much as the role might have had some advantages, at the same time, his wife, I suspect, would have felt frustrated being in a relationship with a man who wouldn't grow up. He worshipped her, but at the same time deep down probably resented the fact that he was not able to be an Adult in the archetypal sense. For her the payoff was possibly the reassurance of being in control. If we are lacking in self-esteem and security, then being in control is a way of dominating our world so we do feel secure. The trouble is we cannot control the world and so this leaves us feeling more insecure (so we try to control things more). As a Parent, we create a Child to allow us to feel in control (secure) yet having a Child, as a partner makes us feel less secure.

Whenever you identify an archetype in yourself that is out of balance, ask yourself what the payoff is for remaining in that state. If you can identify the payoff then you can decide whether it's worth continuing, given the disadvantages.

Bringing the parent and child into balance

To heal the Parent/Child involves working with the Adult, rather than ridiculing the Child when you find it appearing, or feeling ashamed at that Parent of yours. The Child simply is not capable of maturing without the help of the inner Adult. Likewise for the critical Parent, letting go of the domination and control is going to need the Adult's assistance.

Once you have identified which of the two roles you play and in what situations, you can now look for what triggers the Child or Adult to appear. For instance let's say that you find yourself criticizing your partner for not acting the way you believe they should act. You immediately identify your critical Parent on the loose. This gives you a chance to stand back and ask yourself: "what is going on here?" Domination comes from insecurity – trying to control everything to lessen our insecurity. So in this case the Adult may ask themselves: "why am I feeling so insecure?" the Adult is rational and logical and by connecting with this part of ourselves we are able to reason our way through the issue. Likewise if the Child steps back from the emotiveness of the situation and engages with their Adult, they may find that being made to feel responsible, or being criticized triggers their Child. Remember it's more about the WAY things are said and the facial expressions than the actual words. If I sigh loudly, and speak in an irate tone whilst glaring at my partner, even if I say "it's ok" both he and I will know that it is not.

Ask yourself what the payoff is for yourself. After all you would not have stuck with this way of interacting if there was not some benefit in it for yourself. Do you enjoy feeling in control? Is dominating a way of feeling better about who you are? As a Child, not having to be responsible for anything certainly would feel good. If you are not responsible you can never be held accountable. Now that's a payoff!

The more awareness or consciousness we can bring to our actions and behavior, the more our Adult self is able to ask of ourselves: "Is this the way I choose to be?" Through engaging an inner dialogue with our adult we bring about the desired change.

There are however certain instances where one party or both may not be able to access their adult at all as in the case of psychosis, or only periodically as is the case in bipolar disorder (maniac depression).

Note: The Parent /Child is arguably the most common imbalance that occurs in relationships. It is similar to the Tyrant/Rebel and the Perpetrator/Victim. If you find yourself identifying with the Parent/Child, you may find these other archetypal opposites useful.

The dynamics are also found in many other archetypal opposites, such as the Perfectionist and the Slob, where the Perfectionist would also be the disapproving, critical Parent and the Slob, the rebellious, passive aggressive Child or the Tyrant and the Victim, where once again the Tyrant would be an extreme version of the Critical Parent and the Victim, the fearful, abused Child.

Note

1. © alan chapman 2004-2006; Businessballs 1995-2006.
   http://www.businessballs.com/mehrabiancommunications.htm accessed
   15 March 2008

Chapter Nine

The Perfectionist and the Slob

Louise was clearly nervous at our first meeting. She refused to make eye contact, and instead shifted her gaze around the room. The feeling that she emanated was one of fear and uncertainty. I couldn't help noticing her nails, which were bitten down to the skin. She was extremely thin and her pale complexion was drawn with worry lines.

"The problem is that he is a complete couch potato. He never lifts a finger to help in the flat and when I ask him to do so, he tells me to relax and enjoy myself more. But I can't enjoy myself when the ironing is not done and the dishes are piled in the sink. By the time I've done all the housework, he has gone to bed. I am exhausted after working full-time, then doing all the chores. If he wants sex, it's the last thing I want or feel like. Maybe if he helped a bit more, I'd feel less burdened and more willing. He jokes that we have corridor sex, in that we say "F!!* You," when we pass each other in the passage."

Another common archetype pair is the Perfectionist and the Slob. One person will keep their areas of the house meticulously ordered and clean, while their mirror opposite will leave a trail of clothes from the bedroom to the bathroom every night, often without even noticing that they are doing so.

An amusing incident happened when one such Slob decided to give her husband a pleasant Valentine's Day surprise. Coming home early, she removed her clothing, leaving a pathway of clothes as a guide up to the bedroom, where she lay naked under the covers clutching a bottle of champagne ready to leap out on his arrival. Things backfired a little when he came home and ignoring the clothes turned on the TV to catch the latest game. When finally it became clear that in spite of trips to the fridge and toilet, he still had not taken the lingering lingerie into consideration, she polished off the greater part of the champagne alone before going to admonish him. The poor man's response was simply that he was so used to seeing her clothes lying all over the place he ignored them while waiting for her to come home.

The Perfectionist will hover around your near finished plate, ready to whisk it off to the kitchen the moment your fork and knife are placed down. They will scrub and tidy and in extreme cases make relaxing in their homes about as likely as relaxing in the dentist's chair. If every surface is not polished to a glowing shine, if every item is not packed away in its correct place, if there is a spot of dirt on their shirt, they will not be able to relax until they have driven home to change. If the kids' room is a mess they will go to pieces and may even avoid having animals because of the way they shed. Not every Perfectionist is as radical as these examples, and obviously there are degrees of perfectionism and these may alter depending on the circumstances.

On the opposite end of the see-saw is the classic Slob, lying in front of the TV, beer in hand, remote control in the other. Washing lies piled head high in the kitchen, the dustbins haven't been emptied in days and there is a suspicious smell emanating from behind the sofa. Dogs are sprawled on the sofas, and clothes and newspapers are strewn haphazardly across the lounge and bedroom, where the bed stays unmade – once again an extreme version of this archetype. However, you ask, have these two maintained a relationship?

Jason and Katie were perfect examples of the Slob and the Perfectionist cohabiting. The couple had been living together for five years. Jason was your basic slob in the house – everything to do with housework tended to be ignored and left for some never present future, while Katie was a Perfectionist and could not relax until everything was washed, cleaned and in its correct place. Jason would come back from work and head for the couch, and watch TV, seemingly oblivious to Katie's attempts to cook and clean. When finally Katie did collapse in an exhausted heap in front of the telly with Jason, he was hurt and confused when his advances were met with rejection.

The bedroom was no different: - Jason's five undisciplined dogs all piled onto and into the bed, stretching out luxuriously, while the couple teetered on the edges. This did not make for good intimate space. (Often when we are not able to be intimate with others, we substitute intimacy with people for intimacy with pets, who offer little threat of rejection.)

Katie came to me because whilst she did love Jason, she was finding the situation intolerable. Expressing her anger usually resulted in a flaming row and although for a few days Jason might try to alter his slovenly ways, long term saw no real improvement in the situation. Jason on the other hand, could not understand why Katie was so "hung up" on having everything ship shape. It seemed an unnecessary waste of time and energy, which he felt could have been spent together on the sofa.

Jason, having the Child as part of his archetypal makeup, played the part of the naughty/rebellious Child. When Katie was angry with him, he would head off to the pub, leaving Katie fuming at home over the ironing. When he returned several pints later, it was to find Katie on the couch asleep, leaving him to the dubious delight of his mutts. When he was with Katie, he wanted to play with her – have fun, have sex, drink, hang around at clubs etc. Katie, as the Parent was not interested in such frivolities – there was too much to do.

The dynamics of Jason's water and Kate's fire, which flowed into their jobs as well, was understandably cause for much tension, which Jason coped with by withdrawing into the mindless world of TV, as a way of avoiding having to confront Katie's anger, while Katie resentfully ironed and cleaned. After an evening like this, sex was just not going to happen, causing resentment and frustration, this time from Jason. It seemed like the only contented ones were the dogs.

What had originally drawn the couple to each other: i.e. Jason's relaxed approach to life and his ability to have fun and play, were now seen as negatives, while Katie's calm reassurance, responsibility and contentment with taking a backseat when it came to socialising, were viewed now with irritation. Both retreated to either ends of their proverbial see-saw and in doing so, created a greater emotional distance between themselves, to the point that the relationship had a very real chance of ending.

The Payoff

While the payoff for the Slob is not having to take responsibility for the way things are and the joy of indulging in procrastination, at times the Slob may also be using this lack of doing, as a form of passive aggressive behaviour towards the Perfectionist. "If you can't win, make them seriously pissed off," could at times be the principle at play. The Slob may also simply have a lower need for tidiness than the Perfectionist.

The Perfectionist's payoff comes from the satisfaction of achieving neatness. Here is something that can be controlled in a world where the Perfectionist may feel they have very little control. Being busy may also be a way of avoiding deeper issues that need to be addressed. Also, if the home looks neat then that must indicate that all is well, right?

Healing the Slob and Perfectionist

When Katie and Jason realised that they were looking at their mirror opposites, which interestingly they had not been aware of, they started seeing the problems as theirs, as opposed to each others. In other words, both of them accepted that each of them owned a certain amount of the problem. They also understood why they were together. It became easier then for them to realise that waiting for the other to change was going to get them where it had got them to date – precisely nowhere.

Each accepted that the change they wanted in the other, began with them. Jason had to learn to engage with his Adult self and as such help around the place, while Katie needed to let go of her critical Parent and as an Adult, rather than an admonishing Parent, be able to talk about her feelings. Jason soon learnt that a bit of time spent helping, laid the foundations for sex later. Katie eased up on the perfect housewife bit and in time became accepting that their home would not be absolutely spick and span the whole time. She also acknowledged that part of her need for perfection was due to a feeling of lack of self worth. She wasn't perfect, so she had to make her life look as if it was.

On the bed, the dogs had to let the humans take preference, (which did not do their canine egos any good), but after a few nights and a few new doggy baskets, everyone settled down to the new routine. This allowed Jason to actually cuddle up close to Katie and to feel some of the intimacy and reassurance he had been wanting.

The Slob, is not necessarily lazy as such, but just not as concerned with appearances as the Perfectionist is. The Slob has a lower level of when things are just fine, while the Perfectionist is seldom ever happy with the status quo. There is always some dust, some untidiness, some imperfection that needs to be fixed, before the Perfectionist can be happy. What happens then is that the Perfectionist never really can be happy. Why? Simply because to be happy requires perfection and nothing, (at least to the Perfectionist), is ever perfect. The result is an inability to experience real joy.

- Perfection = Joy
- Imperfect = Lack of Joy
- The world is not perfect, therefore there can be no joy.

Above all, the Perfectionists view themselves as imperfect, and often can be very hard on themselves when they perceive that they have been less than perfect (which is pretty much most of the time). This need for everything to be right, creates a very polarised view of right and wrong, which can make accepting that others are not necessarily wrong simply because they don't share your religion, work ethic, race, background and cleaning skills, very hard for the Perfectionist to accept. It's easy to see then, why they would learn the most from a Slob. Deep down, they long to be able to let things go, even if only for a few moments, but their rigid control and belief in what comprise "right and wrong," holds them back. Katie wanted, on some level to be like Jason, (because as we know, that's what lay in her Shadow). Jason's way of getting back at her "Parent," was to do what all teenagers do – make sure his room was untidy, partly because the mess did not concern him, and partly because it was a passive/aggressive way at getting back at "mum."

The Perfectionist then needs to allow themselves to accept that they alone are not right. And that Perfection either exists in all things *as they are*, or in nothing at all. Who can say who is the Perfect man or woman – ask 20 people and you'll get 20 different responses. Perfection then exists only as a concept of acceptance of things being perfect at all times.

Chapter Ten

The Miser and the Big Spender

The archetype of the Miser is a person who believes in lack rather than abundance. As a result, everything and particularly money, is always viewed as being in short supply. So Scrooge will scrimp and save, sometimes getting real pleasure from putting his/her family through hardship, to save a few pennies, even when in actuality there is enough money etc to go around. The Miser may drive across town to get a discount on an item, putting him or herself through great inconvenience for the reward of a few pennies saved. The expectation from the Miser is that his or her partner should share in this outlook and when they don't, sparks inevitably fly.

The Big Spender archetype is often typified in jokes as the woman with a credit card who spends her husband's (his-spend) hard earned income with gay abandon. For her pleasure is gained through the sight of the card being swiped through the machine. The Big Spender, spends with little thought or concern as to what is available. They may buy houses, cars, run up huge hire purchase accounts with little realistic insight as to the real state of their financial affairs. It can be an act of revenge against a partner, as in one woman I knew who would deliberately go and run up huge amounts on her credit card if she was angry with her husband. Unable to really win an argument or confront the situation from her Adult as opposed to Child self, the credit card provided the perfect revenge.

"I want to buy a new pair of stockings but my husband will create a scene if I do, so I'll have to buy them at the supermarket and amongst the list of groceries, he won't notice them." I sat confused. This was the same man who had recently purchased a brand new luxury car for himself. This was one woman's problem with her Miser, while Stephanie was on the other end of the scale: "I was working really hard to earn sufficient to get the kids through school. We had been through a tough time and so I wanted to build up a nest egg. My husband however, saw things differently. After the financial drought he wanted to buy everything he felt we needed. The more I held back the more he spent. It became a constant tug of war between my feeling he was spending unnecessarily and him feeling I was being a Scrooge. Even when it came to home maintenance he would get a quote from one person, without bothering to get a second, reasoning that the extra time wasted would be better spent working and making money rather than trying to save it. Only problem was, he wasn't earning money."

"At some point I sort of called his bluff and started threatening to book overseas holidays etc. It was interesting because it was he then who pulled in the reins. I guess it was a balance thing. The more he spent, the more I held back and when I turned the tables, the reverse happened."

Seldom is there any issue that causes more friction in relationships than money. Whilst money may be the last layer on the onion skin as far as problems in a relationship are concerned, it is the symbol (energetically) of who feels they are putting more into the relationship bank and who feels that their partner may be making serious withdrawals.

Sometimes in relationships, one partner may be the big spender when it comes to large purchases such as exotic cars, overseas holidays and expensive trinkets, but that same person may rant and rave over minor expenditures, such as brands of food, home maintenance and household budgets. Their partner may mirror this in being afraid of large purchases, while happily blowing big bucks on clothes etc.

A businessman I knew would happily spend large amounts of money:– an upmarket second property, an expensive motor vehicle, disco equipment for the kids etc. yet lose his cool over relatively small expenditures by his wife. Consequently the relationship see-sawed between his expenditure and her attempts to recover or manage things to pay for his lifestyle.

Much of the time the Big Spender feels entitled to spend irrespective of whether they actually have the money. "I work hard for money and do a job I dislike, so I deserve to enjoy myself by indulging in a bit of Retail Therapy," is a typical justification for spending. This can become a pattern, in that the minute the Spender is feeling down or depressed, spending becomes a way of attempting to feel good again, the reason no doubt that in bi-polar illness, shopping sprees have become a recognised part of the diagnosis.

"My husband would return with the most outlandish array of purchases, from ornaments, D.I.Y. equipment, books, models, clothing etc most of which seldom ever got taken out of the box." Worse still, some sufferers of bi-polar, believing that at that point they can do no wrong, will make crazy investments, large donations or gifts to organisations or family members and friends, or spend huge sums of money on pornography, prostitution, gambling or holidays and travel, with little regard for the finance that is actually available to them. As they spend more, their partner will naturally draw in the reins ever tighter.

Money as energy

Money is a form of energetic transfer. We use energy to obtain it and we trade that energetic build-up for the energetic results of others' labour. Money gives us power in the outside world or have you not heard the saying that if you are rich and crazy you are eccentric. If you are poor and crazy you are simply crazy.

Money allows us to control people, corporations, organisations and even countries. It is not evil as some would have it, but rather it is our attachment to it that can be seen as evil as it stops our ability to really live.

Notice the Palindrome (words that read backwards and forwards) of evil is live:

EVIL = LIVE

Evil is when we don't live our lives to their fullest potential, when we hold ourselves back from being all we could be.

A wealthy man, who is not attached to his wealth, is free, while a wealthy man, who is obsessed by his wealth, is a prisoner of his own making.

Money = potency

Throughout time, men have traditionally been the hunters, whether bringing home the kill or making a killing, the principle remains the same. Women are gatherers (shoppers or spenders). What happens in relationships then is that when a man is earning (or hunting well) he feels more manly and thus is more potent and active sexually. In a primal lifestyle, as the better hunter he would earn the right to more gatherers/women, being seen as the best bet for procreation and so improve the tribal lineage in terms of better hunters, which would ensure the survival of the tribe. Plus, as owner of more food, he would be more attractive to the gatherers as they instinctively sought out a partner who could provide well for them and their offspring.

Those less fortunate at hunting had to hang around the sidelines and hope for the best of the cast-offs. Consequently their sexual drive would be diminished, as they believed themselves to be unworthy, and saw little hope of pursuing any potential prospects, knowing they would in all likelihood be rejected. Not much has changed, in that the more a man feels he is earning the more sexually active he becomes, while those who have been retrenched or are unable to earn, often find their libido leaving with their cash. This inability to function as a man further wears away at an already frazzled self esteem and the problem spirals downward, unless there is some sort of intervention. Obviously in different class structures and cultures, the actual amount of money considered a good income differs hugely.

An exception to this would be teenagers who are not expected to earn and so would not necessarily link sexuality with cents (or sense for that matter!)

This problem is further enhanced, when the woman is the big earner and the man unemployed or at best earning a meagre income. Very often here the man will be the watery one in the relationship and the female show all the fiery attributes. In one such relationship I observed, it was the woman who went out to the pub with her mates after work and who would arrive home late, while her husband cooked and put the children to bed. In their reversal of traditional earning roles, they had also reversed the traditional social norms.

This is not to say that relationships where the woman out-earns her partner do not work however, in many cases, the role reversal does increase tension and potential for sexual withdrawal on the part of the man, simply because in not being able to remove thousands of years of conscious or subconscious programming which states that men are the hunters, he simply feels less of a man. And the woman, after generations of suppression and domination, steps into a new level of power at the very moment he is feeling that his power has been withdrawn.

Money as control

If you are familiar with the Eastern concept of chakras (energy centres situated throughout the body), you will know that in the second chakra, situated below the navel, are, amongst other things, situated the seat of money and sex, which is why the two are so often intertwined. Both can be used to control others. The partner who does the major earning may use money as a means of control and manipulation of the other, while that party may use sex (in withholding or rewarding through sex) as a means to balance or retaliate against the control.

Often in divorces, money is used as a means to humiliate or manipulate the other partner or as a means to coerce a partner who wants to leave, into staying.

The Payoff

What motivates the Miser to withhold cash?

What advantages does the Big Spender receive from blowing bucks?

Is the Miser insecure and hoarding wealth offers an opportunity to stave off that fear? Ask yourself: "how much is enough?" Often extremely wealthy people still carry an inherent belief that they don't have enough, even when logic would dictate that unless they acted extremely foolishly, they would have enough to cover their expenses in this life time many times over. The Miser can also indicate a deeper emotional hoarding: - when we are too afraid to share or expose our emotions we hold them in check, afraid to share ourselves with others. Hoarding may be a way of avoiding opening ourselves up to others and life in general.

Ever been in a bar when one guy always seems to be buying the rounds? Often having a low self esteem, the instant popularity he enjoys as a result, makes him (or her) feel better about themselves, problem being when the money runs out... so do the "friends."Money can't buy us love, yet we often confuse its power with the ability to buy love and respect. Spending money on others, may make us feel better about who we are and may allow us to feel more powerful. Spending money in wild shopping sprees often reduces tension and stress and makes us feel more powerful, until we face the debts we cannot pay. (Wild spending sprees are also linked to bipolar depression.)

Balancing the Miser and the Big Spender

In the archetypes of the Miser and the Big Spender, can be found the controlling Parent and the irresponsible Child. The Miser (as the Parent) needs to learn to let go of fear and control and replace a lack mentality with an abundance belief system. They also need to learn how to share not only their wealth, but also themselves. The rewards for giving in terms of feelings of well-being, have been documented in research done by Psychologist Elizabeth Dunn at the University of British Columbia. She found that giving money away to charity etc made for happier people.[1]

The Child-like Big Spender, needs to assume more responsibility for their lives in general and realise that the security money appears to buy is not true security – investments crumble, houses halve in value, exchange rates fluctuate, none of which we can control. The more they rebel in the face of this then, the greater problems they face long term, creating more insecurity and thus tension/stress and the desire to spend to overcome this. It's a cyclical pattern. Its not that generosity per se is bad – quite the opposite, its when it is done with ulterior motives such as buying love, wanting to look good or as a retaliation against a partner's stinginess, that its out of balance.

Through the generosity of the Miser and the discipline of the irresponsible Child, these extremes can be brought into harmonious balance.

Closely linked to the psyche of the Miser and Big Spender, is the Priest and prostitute.

Note

1. www.mg.co.za/.../breaking_news/breaking_news__business/
   &articleid=335263&referrer=RSS accessed 30 March 2008-03-30
   University of B.C. psychologist Elizabeth Dunn. Even spending $5 in the right way can make you happier.
   Ms. Dunn and her colleagues – UBC grad. Student Lara Aknin and Harvard researcher Michael Norton – designed and conducted a survey on money, happiness and giving. They found greater happiness among people who give money to charity and buy gifts for friends, regardless of income.

Chapter Eleven

The Priest and the Prostitute

The traditional archetypal view of a Priest is usually that of a celibate man, often intense, devoted to his cause, intelligent but in his shadow, possibly perverse, lacking joy, a recluse and possibly out of touch with the reality of day to day living, having never experienced marriage etc. The Priest is the stoic – the one who suffers in silence, believing that in some way that is his/her noble fate. (In this way there are overlaps with the Martyr archetype.)

He may be compassionate or lacking in any emotional expression. The Priest believes he (or she because archetypes are not gender specific), should be behaving in a certain moralistic way and frowns upon the extravagances, emotional or physical of others. He assumes power in a relationship by withdrawing to his own inner church where the world of nastiness and reality is excluded. Through this practise others often experience Priests as judgemental. They also frequently deny their own needs completely for the sake of family and their partner, as a priest does for his vocation.

The Prostitute, on the other hand, (and I am using the word in an archetypal rather than literal interpretation), exchanges her sense of self for material or emotional gain. She (and once again in reality she may be the man in the relationship), will go against her own better judgement in order to reap a reward. Integrity then becomes a commodity to trade, leaving the Prostitute with a reduced sense of self-worth each time the transaction occurs. You seduce a partner not because you are attracted to them, but rather for what they can offer in return. This partner does not have to be a sexual one, it may be your business partner, or your creative potential, such as someone in advertising who remains in the business never fulfilling their creative potential, simply because they are seduced themselves by large pay packages, power and company perks.

The Prostitute will in the extreme expression sell their very soul for financial and or other security. This is the person who may spend years hating what they do, but through financial fear, will be unwilling to let go of the position or relationship and establish something that is closer to their goal or ideal.

I recall for many years working for a particular client in advertising whose account constituted 80 percent of my income. The nature of the work was completely boring, uncreative and uninspiring, with completely unrealistic deadlines and constant changes, that made any routine extremely difficult, which given the fact that I had a baby and a toddler to look after was a problem. Yet for almost ten years I remained locked into this relationship, simply because it paid the bills. Now there is nothing wrong with that, if one can detach oneself from the situation and from ones frustration and anger and find inspiration elsewhere, (i.e. its simply a means to help support a more inspiring end).

I wanted to leave, I really did, but the fear of lack and the jingle of cash was more powerful than the feeling of being frustrated and unfulfilled. It was only when my "angels," got tired of my behaviour, that they forced the relationship to end. Two weeks later I had the idea for my first book, and I have never looked back. Maybe I needed all those years to reach that point, its not really important, what is, is how grateful I am to the supposedly "unfair," processes/people that brought about the change. (Thank-you, Thank-you!)

Whenever the prostitute is in our relationships, know that we are selling ourselves short in some way. Most of all we sell our integrity for some reward. Think about this in terms of people such as corrupt cops or Government officials, who sell their personal integrity for financial gain or the promise of power.

Often, just when we believe we have transformed an archetype, we get tested by the universe. Naturally then, no sooner had I declared that I was out of advertising for good and ready to follow my heart, I got offered an extremely lucrative contract, that to my Prostitute was most seductive.

To the extent we prostitute ourselves, is the extent that we lose our self esteem.

Over the years, there is not much shocks me when it comes to working with people – I have encountered many human failings (my own included) in many forms, however, this client really did surprise me:- here was a good-looking, well educated, wealthy man, who was telling me in a matter of fact manner, how, on discovering his wife was having an affair with his best friend, had not confronted her angrily as one might have expected. Instead, he had taken her out on a lavish date, given her flowers and over a glass of imported bubbly, whilst cuddled up with her on the couch later, had told her that he knew what was going on.

Most men in a similar situation would have reacted very differently you'll agree! And I have to admit I don't think my approach would have been quite the same. This was an intriguing reaction. He also revealed that this was only one of a long list of infidelities during their 10 year marriage. Not only was he the sole breadwinner, but he had put up with her affairs for many years, and had also accepted the role of cook and chief carer for their three children. Her life seemed to focus on expensive hair appointments and socialising.

In his constant rescuing of her, his stoicism, his image as the "good guy," and his lack of emotional expression, his almost celibate marriage (she was not happy to extend her favours at home,) and his withdrawal into the monastery of his office, he showed himself to be the archetypal priest (close to sainthood one could argue!) She, as the Prostitute, sold herself for attention rather than money: she loved the excitement, the thrill of illicit encounters, the intrigue of sex in forbidden places and the appreciation of an admiring lover.

The "badder," she became the more addicted he was to her badness, while he became ever more stoic and priest like. She revealed that she found his lack of emotional expression a problem and blamed this for her adulterous encounters. In truth they were swinging further apart and creating ever more havoc as they did so. She wondered how bad she had to be for him to stop being "good," and react.

There were also elements of the Child (her) and the Parent (him) in their relationship. It was a desperately sad and unhappy situation and I felt huge compassion for them and the trap they had created for themselves.

The Payoff

The payoff for the Prostitute is security, money, prestige, holding onto a partner or to rise above a previous more impoverished life - its integrity vs physical or financial survival or reward. However, there is another dimension to it; the Prostitute seduces and controls those who he/she uses as "clients." Because the Prostitute has little self esteem, she/he seeks to control his/her world through the manipulation of others. The Prostitute is "bought," but the balance is that while her "client," believes he/she has bought her, he/she are themselves being controlled, so who really holds the power?

Sex and money are two very powerful controlling forces and the Prostitute can use them to his/her advantage. What do many cults do to new recruits? Persuade them to hand over their money in large quantities and often offer them free sex. Over and over again, ex cult members reveal how they were pressured into handing over large sums of money and were often threatened with blackmail if they tried to leave. The blackmail usually revolves around revealing some of the sexual practices that they had partaken of during their involvement with the cult.

Healing the Priest and the Prostitute

To heal, the Priest would need to come down from his lofty intellectual height and start engaging with his/her emotions. (The Priest is far more comfortable intellectualising emotions rather than feeling them). Withdrawing into a world that renounces the unpleasantness of day to day relationship squabbles is his/her defence. He or she needs to drop the need to look good, while denying emotions such as anger etc. The Priest needs to discover that its alright to have emotions – being human involves enjoyment of earthly delights, rather than renouncing them.

The Prostitute's awareness of his/her archetype, will allow for conscious assessment of a situation: "I've been offered a contract for six weeks, the work doesn't inspire me, but it will create sufficient income to allow me to do what does inspire me for a couple of months after that. It seems a fair trade then – six weeks for eight weeks." Issues such as: "I'm in a loveless marriage to a wealthy man who has married me simply for my looks – as a trophy really. Do I accept the comfortable privileged lifestyle and ignore his other liaisons and my dislike of having sex with him? Is this a situation I want to remain in for the rest of my life?" Knowing we are working with the Prostitute archetype allows us to make conscious decisions rather than act unconsciously.

Being a Prostitute as such is not "bad," anymore than being a Priest is "good." Both can serve us and both can stifle our growth according to how aware we are of them and how we use the strengths and weaknesses in each.

Note

In historical times many of what we now refer to as prostitutes, were in actuality very powerful temple guardians, who used sex as a tool to allow the kundalini or snake like energy in each person to rise from the base of the spine upwards and in so doing to heal the person or extend their spiritual development. These women were definitely not selling themselves for money and although they may have had a great knowledge of sex, can hardly be viewed as prostitutes as such.

Chapter Twelve

The Be-er and the Do-er

Storm liked to get things done.

In the pursuit of this she drove herself mercilessly to achieve, working day and often night, seldom taking breaks, often to the point of delaying going to the toilet while she sat at her computer getting just another thing done. Her husband, Mike, on the other hand was very laid back. He was self-employed and worked in his own time when it suited him. Tomorrow was just as good as today.

Given that the couple had their own business the combination was understandably volatile. Mike simply could not understand why Storm worked so hard. If money was coming in, was the extra work and effort really worth a few more pounds? He longed to be able to spend more time with her in a non working situation. Storm on the other hand was always too busy completing just one more job or writing just one more invoice. They each had a car, not the latest models it must be said, but sufficient for their needs. They also had a bond free house and enough to pay for their children's school fees and general housekeeping with sufficient to be able to afford small luxuries such as occasionally eating out and family holidays. For most couples a lifestyle independent of bosses, corporate politics and the need to fight through traffic every morning would be ideal. Yet they were not happy.

Storm resented his easy lifestyle, the daily naps he took after lunch, his ability to say "no" and procrastinate, while she, playing the role of "little Miss Efficiency," toiled on. As is often the case when women bear resentment, they withdraw emotionally and sexually. This causes frustration and resentment from the man who not realising that there is or why there might be resentment, can't understand why his wife or partner has become frigid. Like most couples in this situation they would have moments when all seemed well, (based on his performance level in the home with chores and at work with production), but for the most part they were drifting further and further apart. Storm's monthly bookclub provided an outlet where she, together with the other women, could gripe and moan about their errant spouses, before returning to a world where intimacy did not exist.

The problem, in her mind was clearly about him, rather than herself. It was obvious wasn't it? She was the one doing all the work and he was clearly the slacker. How could she be at fault? Mike was extremely happy with his life in all aspects other than his relationship with his wife. He had achieved all he had hoped for, without having to sell his soul for it. If only Storm could be as happy and content as he was and not drive herself so hard, life at last, after so many years of dodgy business partners and failing companies, would be bliss.

The Payoff

Storm's payoff was simple: being a Martyr, she could hang on the cross of her own design, in order to receive the sympathy of others. In being the Do-er she felt herself to be the noble heroine, fighting against the odds to win. (One of the main odds, was naturally Mike). "Shame, poor thing," her book club members would say each month as she told the latest update. "Shame," was the regular response from her family who had started to resent Mike. Seen to be sacrificing herself, was the payoff for Storm. The harder she worked, the more acknowledgements she would receive from others and the more this would feed her sense of self.

Healing the Be-er and Do-er

Storm's lesson was to move from being the Martyr/Do-er into the Warrior, able to confront her feelings and to stand up for herself in the relationship. Boundaries needed to be drawn and responsibilities shared. She also had to let go of control and start trusting and entrusting Mike to take more of her responsibilities, even if he did them in a different way to her. Looking at why she couldn't trust anyone other than herself was a big step towards healing her wounds. She also had to look at issues of her own self worth and why she needed her work to feel good about herself. As she worked at developing self worth, she came to feel worthy of time out and enjoyment.

Working also staved off a deep fear and insecurity that stemmed from a lack of trust. Having had her trust shattered as a child, Storm found it hard to trust another person to be responsible for an income. As long as she worked, things would be alright. If she handed that responsibility over to Mike, she would have to trust him to provide and that's where her subconscious stepped in and replayed her old program: "you can't trust anyone."

Taking on more responsibility was hard for Mike, but through doing so, he began to trust and respect himself more, which had a positive influence on his work. The respect he gained from Sue also helped him to adapt more to his new role.

Chapter Thirteen

The Tyrant, the Rebel and the Victim

"Every time the woman from the bank calls (which is about three times a month) to clear funds coming into my account, she asks me what it's for. Her manner though is so cold, almost reproachful and very officious. Each time I want to say something absolutely outrageous (instead of it's simply a business transaction), like: its payment for an internet video of myself masturbating, or it's for the sale of sex toys - anything just to shake her up a bit." This is an example of the Rebel archetype wanting to emerge.

David is the boss of the family (as he is quick to remind everyone.) As such, he controls everything at the office and in the home. Mary, his wife gets an allowance for household expenses, which is strictly monitored by David. (And he is quick to query expenses and to remonstrate with Mary over amounts he feels are not justified, even though they are very well moneyed.) Mary has become a slave to his rules and is afraid to stand up to him or confront him in any way. An employee of 11 years has been found to have been stealing from him. He is outraged at this disloyalty. David believes he is a good man – a caring husband and consistent employer. Isn't he the one who goes to work each day? Why should things at home not be shipshape after all? If the dog has done a turd on the garden path, if a cup is out of place, in fact if everything is not "perfect," on his homecoming, David explodes into a wild rage, (while Mary cowers in the kitchen).

David has recently had a heart attack and has been told to slow down or preferably stop working. This has caused a major upset for him, as he has to face the prospect of being at home a lot more, if not full time. Suddenly he feels afraid, no longer the powerful man in charge. He realises he doesn't really know his wife as a person as such, only an implementer of his wishes. His children are estranged. His kingdom is crumbling and for the first time in his life, he has no clue what to do.

David is a typical Tyrant. He needs to dominate and control. If he is not dominating and controlling, he fears that his world will crumble, as it is currently doing. Afraid, he believes more control will solve the problem, yet it requires more energy. He is tired, exhausted in fact from having to control everything and every-one in his life. He suspects he may even be depressed, which is a major admission of failure for him.

When David came to see himself as assuming the role of a Tyrant, he was genu-inely surprised. He believed that this was how all "real" men should behave. He had been brought up by his own tyrannical father this way and had as a result completely cut himself off from his feminine, watery side – his Dad would not have tolerated any "sissy" behaviour. He could not ever recall crying and if an uncomfortable emotion arose, he would suppress it immediately (with the exception of anger). Yet he could see that this behaviour had not worked. His staff were clearly rather pleased that his departure was imminent. He realised that he had mistaken subservience for loyalty and he could understand that anyone who had challenged (rebelled) against his au-thority had quickly been ousted and branded as a troublemaker. All that were left now were resentful (withdrawing) compliant staff who were archetypal Children.

Worse still he admitted realising that his wife did not love him, rather she feared him, and withdrew, particularly in the bedroom. His only son became the rebellious Child, in his father's eyes, by entering into a homosexual relationship, which he flaunted in front of his father. David viewed his son's sexual preference as a huge betrayal of the time and effort he had put into his son and his proposed future in the company. His son had to be a man, just as he was. Yet here was his son throwing it all away, to enter the theatre, of all places, with no certainty of financial security and a pouting ponce as a lover to boot. It was too much for Da-vid to deal with and he had refused to have any communication with his son for ten years. (Can you see how the son was mirroring the opposite of his fiery father, in exploring his watery/feminine nature?) This son was the perfect way for David to have balance. When David could see (for he was an intelligent man,) that his son, rather than simply being rebellious and wanting to hurt David, was actually partially a product of David's own suppressed nature, David started to heal and stop living in anger and blame. He was later reunited with his son.

David also actually started encouraging his wife to develop her own interests as opposed to thwarting them. As she did, he started respecting her more, and her self esteem grew. A breakthrough experience was the day David, in understanding why his son had to rebel, allowed himself to cry. It was a wonderful indication of just how much he had shifted and he reported feeling better than he had for many years. Under the guidance of his physician, he was able to reduce and later stop taking his anti depression tablets. I salute his courage in facing his demons. He also showed me that it's never too late to be happier and to work with one's issues.

The Tyrant needs to be in control, because it's the only way they can stave off their own feelings of insecurity. They may spend their lives bullying their partner, because deep down they fear that unless they do so, the partner may leave. The more worthless the partner is, the less likely they will have the personal power and finance to seek a happier relationship. Tyrants are often cowards – desperately seeking dominion through fear over others, so that they can avoid confronting their own fears. The only defence their Victim has is either to withdraw or to rebel.

The Tyrant thrives on the fear he or she creates in others, while their partner is afraid of what will happen if the Tyrant's needs are not pandered to. If the right meal is not cooked, if the job is not done just the way they want it, irrespective if they did not convey the information in the first place, all could lead to a violent outburst and humiliation for the Victim. They can go from being completely normal to a wild raging beast in a matter of seconds, most often for the smallest of issues and conversely, can remain calm when one would have thought they had been provoked. This unpredictability makes them hard to live with, as one constantly spends time trying to second guess their every reaction, which of course empowers them more.

Sometimes the children of Tyrants can grow up to be highly intuitive, as their survival relies on being able to tune into the mood of the Tyrant, in order to sense when an explosion is likely, so they can make themselves scarce or take appropriate avoidance action.

In the Tyrant's world, they reign supreme - everything is about them. Woe betides anyone who tries to usurp this position. This will cause the Tyrant to unleash their most nasty force. Even if the Tyrant may seem to be concerned for the well being of others, for the most part, it disguises an obsession with the self. There is no pain as bad as the Tyrants, no suffering quite as harsh as theirs, no life as hard as what they have to endure. Most often they simply can't view life from any other position but their own, which makes Tyrants one of the more challenging archetypes when it comes to change. Because of their unwillingness to move forward, the tyrant can also be a master at dragging up the past. Incidents long since forgotten by you, may be hauled out of the proverbial closet, to remind the Rebel or Victim, just how tough life has been for them and just how much to blame for their unhappy life they are.

This doesn't mean that when not in this archetype Tyrants aren't nice people, of course they can have many redeeming traits and the Tyrant may only arise in certain relationships and for the rest of the time, the person can be kind, generous, nurturing, caring and have a host of other positive traits. However, all this can change, when their Tyrant archetype emerges leaving those around them dazed, afraid and confused. It is very often their closest relationships that brings out the worst in them, naturally they will seek a Victim or a Rebel to balance their behaviour, but may not experience this extreme in other relationships.

If the Tyrant gains power through fear, the Victim gains power through their Victim status. If I say I had a hard upbringing, then the Victims will be sure to relate a more miserable scenario. If you have lost your job, the Victim is in a worse position because they are being abused in the workplace, while you are free to come and go as you please. Not all Victims take things to this extreme, but the potential is there in each of us, because on some level we all carry this archetype within us.

"I am so afraid of my brother-in-law," a woman revealed, "I am never sure when he is going to explode and create a ghastly scene about something really trivial, so I end up simply agreeing with anything and everything he says to maintain peace. I hate myself for not having the courage to confront and challenge him, even when he deliberately tries to provoke me by saying something loaded or hurtful, but it just seems easier to withdraw."

Here is an example of a Tyrant manipulating and controlling those around him through fear. This fear others have of them, gives the Tyrant power. We can see this throughout the world wherever a Tyrant rules a country. People follow, not through loyalty but because they fear the consequences for not doing so.

Robert Mugabe's reign of terror in Zimbabwe is a classic example of a Tyrant's rule. Anybody who is suspected of supporting an opposition party simply gets intimidated and in many instances killed (at least 20,000 Ndebele people in Matabeleland during 1982 and 1986 alone were killed by his troops and so-called war veterans).[1] After the 2008 elections many more people were tortured and killed as punishment for not voting for him and to intimidate them prior to the re-run of the elctions). While he lives the life of a king and his wife's international shopping sprees are well renowned, his people starve and his economy's inflation spirals out of all control and a once thriving country is brought into misery and despair because of one man's actions. His actions are nothing new, and as we know, history is littered with Tyrants.

What is left for the people then to balance his hold on the country? Either to remain Victims (which is what has been happening), or to Rebel. The trouble is both archetypes, necessitate the Tyrant remaining in power as a Tyrant needs a Rebel or Victim to remain in power.

South Africa was transformed when Victim and Tyrant started communicating as Adults. Through the leaders letting go of the archetypes that had seen them locked in combat, they were able to transcend the situation. However, each time now, years later, the phrase "victim of apartheid" is bandied around, and each time a Tyrant creeps into some position in the government, where they can abuse others, the possibility to swing back into a situation of Tyrant and Victim occurs. (Even though they may now be of the same race group).

That is why by recognising these patterns within ourselves, and transcending them, we in turn create the potential to transform whole countries.

The Rebel needs a Tyrant. Otherwise there would be nothing to rebel against. Whenever in my life I play the Rebel, I create a Tyrant - someone I am afraid of -someone who wants control and power over me. The trouble is I rather like my Rebel. It's got me to explore new avenues of thought, styles of painting and ideas in writing. In being the black sheep, I have been able to find out who I am away from the family flock. The cost has come with having to deal with the inevitable Tyrant.

We often see the Tyrant and the Rebel played out in relationships with our children: "I allowed my adolescent daughter to go with her friends to buy a top for herself, for a party that was coming up. I gave her the money and she went off to the shops with her friends. I was furious when she returned with a black sequined top. It was totally unsuitable for a thirteen year old and she knows I have this thing about black clothes on kids."

What has happened here? The mother has assumed the role of the Tyrant in the teenager's eyes. She is controlling and dominating. The teenager, in experiencing the tyrannies of her mother, finds a way to rebel by buying exactly what she knows will anger her mother and yet, on the surface she has done no actual wrong as such, in that she stuck to the price limit and did indeed spend the money on a top.

Had the mother moved into her nurturing mother role as opposed to the critical tyrannical role, she may have encouraged her daughter's attempts to be independent and responsible by organising her own clothing. Chances are then that the child would not have seen this as an opportunity to rebel, and brought something more appropriate. Even if she had not, the mother may have accepted that tastes have changed and that by allowing her daughter to express her individuality, she would be encouraging her child to develop a sense of self.

The Payoff for the Tyrant

Just what is the benefit in playing the role of Tyrant?

The answer is simple: Control.

The Tyrant attempts to overcome some his/her own fears by witnessing them in others. In other words, by creating fear in another they mirror their own experience which creates a feeling of power which then staves off their own fear. Much of this fear revolves around the person who they are intimidating, leaving them.

Like any shadow ruler, the Tyrant is afraid of loosing power, and so attempting to dominate and manipulate those around him/her is a way to attempt to remain in power. The Tyrant is very insecure and the only way to keep insecurity at bay is to rule supreme. Any attempt to challenge the Tyrant is seen as a direct attack on the self and is met with harsh retaliation.

However, all this control comes at a price and the Tyrant frequently may feel drained and exhausted – it's just so tiring trying to control the world, especially when the world won't always listen!

The Payoff for the Rebel

The Rebel, like the Tyrant may also suffer from low self esteem. Rebelling is a way of making ones mark upon the world - of rebelling against the forces that make one feel small and inadequate. It's a way of saying: "Look, recognise me and my difference."

In order to grow beyond the limitations of our childhood we must rebel to find our own paths. However, there are different ways of rebelling, some that are peaceful and yet powerful for example, Siddhartha or Buddha, who rebelled against the wealth and opulence of his background to live amongst the poor. This rebellion against all he knew, created an environment where he could reach a supreme state of being. In the shadow Rebel, the rebellion can cause chaos, disharmony and at its worst, violence.

In rebelling, the Rebel attempts to gain back the power that has been taken from him/her. However as they do so, they put fear into the Tyrant who then retaliates by becoming more tyrannical.

The Payoff for the Victim

The Victim gets emotional currency from remaining a Victim. The more miserable life becomes, the more, through confiding in others, they can legitimately feel self-pity. This desire for the attention of others, becomes in itself addictive.

I recall playing this Victim game with my husband some years ago. When returning from work, each of us would sit down and relate our day. Whatever unpleasant had happened to the one, had to be surpassed by the other, until all positive and enjoyable experiences were overlooked, in a competitive attempt to win the "I've had the worst day," sympathy prize. Our Tyrants were our employers. The more our expectations were that they were going to behave unreasonably, the more they complied with these expectations. The trouble was it was unfulfilling for both of us. We were both sitting at the bottom end of the see-saw, wanting the other to act as the Adult and support us. When this did not happen, we both became angry and upset Children.

It's unpleasant having to face the reality that one is indeed a Victim and worse still that there is a part of you that wants to remain there. Over the years I have seen clients deliberately sabotage situations where their Victim status was threatened. They were determined to remain there, because the currency it gave them appeared more rewarding than the promise of moving from Victim to Victor.

To move away from being a Victim, means that we may no longer feel at home with our friends who are also playing Victim roles and where we can sit and commiserate with each other about our unfortunate lot in life. I have known many people playing this role who have money, a good job, health etc and yet the desire to see life as being miserable constantly remains. Other Victim role players do not enjoy a happy, upbeat person and they will do all in their power to reduce that person to their Victim status. Consequently to change from a Victim role may not be appealing, as to do so may mean making many other changes in life, most importantly the people you hang out with.

Self-help books, workshops, therapists, all manner of input may be useless, if the desire to remain a victim is there. Caroline Myss, in her book, *Why People Don't Heal And How They Can,* describes this phenomena in depth.

Healing the Victim - How does the Victim become the Victor?

Like so many healings, the healing of these archetypes centres around self-worth. The more a Tyrant feels worthy within themselves, the less the need will be to dominate and control others because they feel insecure. The more a Victim starts to believe in themselves and that they deserve a more respectful relationship, the more they will stand up to those who abuse them or move on.

Self-worth though is not won externally, but rather with experiencing the power of their word. (Otherwise every Miss World, movie star or pop idol, would be comfortable with who they were, and the trash magazines let us know that this is definitely not so). It's when we step by step, start setting goals which we work with integrity to achieve. As we do so it adds to our self esteem. We learn to live with integrity, foremost to themselves. Our word is. If a person does not live in integrity, it's a sure sign that they don't value themselves sufficiently to do so. The more we live in integrity, the greater our self-worth. It's that simple! So the Tyrant will not do as he/she says he will do, while expecting others to do so. Neither will the Victim or the Shadow Rebel live by what they say they will do.

To the extent you are out of integrity is the extent to which your ego is in charge. The more you are in integrity, the more your ego is diminished and your true, higher self can shine through.

The Victim, feels hopeless about life. His/her relationships always seem to end in some form of abuse. He/she has a knack of picking up men or women who he/she feels sorry for and whom he/she feels he/she can reform. After a few months of romance, the inevitable arguments start as well as the abuse (verbal and/or physical), which worsens as time goes on. As a result, he/she starts valuing him/herself less and less until, he/she feels that she may only be worthy of a relationship like this. Afraid to leave the Tyrant, he/she has little means of his/her own or people he/she feels she can reach out to. The Tyrant has got him/her where he/she feels most powerful.

Feeling worthless, the Victims' resolves to change the situation crumble almost as fast as he/she makes them. They feel that they have no power in the world. If we look further into the Victims' world we find that these un-kept resolves, filter out into other aspects of his/her life: into appointments not kept or for which she may be late. Exercise programs not adhered to, diets disintegrated into feel good fast food and so on.

The way out of the maze would be to start making goals, (physical, mental, work related, personal etc) and sets dates and times by which to achieve them. They needn't be huge goals, in fact simple ones such as: "I'll write the letter I have been meaning to write," or "I'll tidy the spare bedroom," or "exercise for 30 minutes twice a week" or "pay all the bills by the end of the month," or "read the book I've been meaning to." Each time he/she achieves these goals, the Victim starts to build his/her self –esteem. As they do so, they are prepared to set more challenging goals. The trick to developing self-esteem is to do what you say you will do by when you say you will do it.

Now a magical thing starts to occur. The Victim starts to believe in themselves. Their worthiness grows as does their personal power. The Tyrant may feel the change and attempt to hold the Victim back, but the Victim now is able to understand the game being played and not be drawn into it. As they become less of a Victim the Tyrant's abuse no longer holds the same fear. The Victim has stepped from the Victim (Child) into the Adult.

Another aspect of healing the Victim will need to engage with, is to face their own Tyrant, locked away in their shadow selves. As we are victimised our inner Tyrant grows. To heal fully then we need to acknowledge and accept that part of ourselves. So often when people who have been victimised and who don't do inner healing work, find themselves in positions of power, they become the very Tyrants they despised. If you feel you may be a Victim, look for where you may be being a Tyrant. (You may need the help of a professional to do this, as often it can be hard to see this shadow aspect of ourselves.) Simply acknowledging that the potential lies within you, is a big step towards healing. If you are victimised at home by a Tyrant, you may find that at work, you give those who report to you a bad time.

Spend some time reflecting back on your life to see where you have acted like a Tyrant. Acknowledge this. Ask for forgiveness if necessary. Then release yourself from guilt, because you now understand why it was that way. Look for other such instances and do the same. This in itself is an empowering process.

Healing for the Tyrant

Healing for the Tyrant is harder, for the following reasons:

1. The Tyrant does not want to let go of power
2. The Tyrant is seldom able to accept responsibility for anything that he/she sees as a failure

Robert Mugabe lost to the rival MDC party in Zimbabwe in the 2008 election. Instead of conceding defeat gracefully, he refused to release the election results. Only weeks later when his cronies had had plenty of time to tamper with the ballots did he decide to have a recount and later a re-run of the elections. No-one could be fooled that the recount would hold the slightest credibility or be representative of the people's decision. However, such was his desire to hold onto power that he lost all reason. At the same time he mobilized his troops and gangs of thugs to terrorise and "punish," those people who were in opposition to his party.

The Tyrant has to be right. He/she is after all in charge. Counselling often proves a challenge, as it requires that one accept at least some of the responsibility for ones actions and has the desire to heal, which many Tyrants aren't able to access. Deep down the Tyrant fears being a Victim. He or she fears the failure that they perceive goes with that archetype and so will fight tooth and nail to not have to face that aspect of themselves and will rather project it onto others.

Gary knew on one level that he had never done anything in his life which he felt constituted success. (He was a middle manager in a sports goods company, but his attitude meant that he seldom remained in any position for any length of time, all of which he attributed to being the fault of those who employed him.) Rather he had ridden on the success of his wife's success in IT. Yet when meeting them socially, it was he who boasted about their material success and at home he was the Tyrant, belittling her notable achievements and gloating on her failures.

Interestingly enough Gary would go on at length about his "successful" mother - her beauty, charm, her intelligence, her degrees and her wealth. In fact his mother had been neither successful not particularly bright, although she had inherited the family fortune (which she had quickly squandered). In not being able to face up to his mother's failings, he had projected them onto his successful wife, making her the failure in spite of her success. He was so addicted to this illusion that any challenges to the nature of reality were met with a hostile and volatile response. His mother was everything and his wife was nothing and he was determined to maintain the illusion.

Gary did not want his mother to fail, because then he would have to access his own feelings of failure, which was too terrifying to do. Ruling was his only defence against his inadequacy. Any confrontation which he didn't "win" or prove to himself how right he was, pushed him into confronting his Victim self, which being afraid, like a cornered dog, he responded to with anger. As such he was a deeply unhappy person, despite the material wealth in his life.

However, there are cases where facing their major fear, i.e. of being left or dethroned, Tyrants do evaluate their lives and do make changes. As their confidence and self-worth develop, their need to rule diminishes.

Healing for the Rebel

How does the Rebel find ways to express this archetype in a constructive, as opposed to destructive manner?

The more a rebel feels good about who they are, the more they will be able to challenge their own shadow, rather than the shadow sides of others.

Rebellion is about expansion. Tyranny is about constriction.

Under a rule of tyranny, societies will eventually constrict and collapse, because constriction sets in motion the opposite force of expansion i.e. rebellion.

However, as we see in many parts of the world, rebels can in time, start adapting the traits of the Tyrants they have deposed, which will in turn create a need for another rebellion, against them. So we can see that this situation is out of balance and creates chaos as a result.

As in the other archetypes described, to heal the Rebel needs to access his/her own Tyrant.

Ask yourself the questions:

• Where have I constricted others?
• Where am I holding or have held others back from reaching their desire or potential?
• When have I tried to control and dominate?

As you answer these questions for yourself, you may experience a feeling of understanding and warmth towards your Tyrant. This may arise when you acknowledge that their behaviour is in you and a projection of you and therefore there is nothing in reality to forgive them for. They were playing a necessary role in your life which you created. In releasing them, you release your own shadow need to constrict, dominate and control others.

Note

1. BBC news 7 May 2008 http://news.bbc.co.uk/2/hi/africa/7388214.stm
   And **humanitarian news and analysis**
   UN Office for the Coordination of Humanitarian Affairs http://www.irinnews.org/
   Report.aspx?ReportId=64321

Chapter Fourteen

The Success and the Failure

Joan had started off as a secretary in the typing pool of a large chain store. She had gradually worked her way up through the ranks and was now one of three Fashion buyers for the chain - a job that offered prestige, travel and a healthy pay packet. When she had married Graham, he, like she once had, held a relatively lowly position in an electronics firm, a position that he still found himself in.

Six years on in their marriage, tension was starting to show. His lack of achievement sat opposite her success. She became irritated with him and spoke to him in a patronising, demeaning way. He sought to enhance his lack of self worth through a string of ill disguised affairs. One evening in a trendy Italian restaurant, they sat in hostile silence until she brought up his latest infidelity. His response was non apologetic and basically along the lines of "she's not frigid and she's available to be with me."

Furious, she got up to leave the restaurant and as she did so deposited his entire plate of Tagliatelle Arrabiata, on top of his head. She marched out – the triumphant woman scorned, as the sauce dripped down his face and body much to the entertainment of the other patrons. Not unexpectedly the relationship ended in divorce.

Then an interesting thing happened. Graham left his job and started his own company. Within months it was flying, and so was he – all round the country winning new clients. Two years later he was a multi-millionaire. She on the other hand had been retrenched when the chain decided to close a number of stores. She had to accept a position in another company far less prestigious and well paid than she had been used to. He was now the Success and she felt herself the Failure. She wanted him back, but he was having way too much fun to revisit an unhappy relationship from the past.

To understand this dynamic of failure and success in a relationship means we have to determine what success actually is.

Is it:

- Happiness?
- Wealth?
- Position?
- Power?
- Academic achievement?
- A good marriage?
- Children?
- Physical fitness?
- Assisting others?
- Beauty?
- Spiritual evolvement?
- Marrying into money/power/position?
- Sporting prowess?
- Peace?
- Travel?
- Lovers?
- Time-out?

I suspect to each person, success is something very different. Yet in relationships, we expect that what we view as success must be shared by our partner, so if you see financial gain as the mark of success, your partner's view that spiritual evolvement is the hallmark of a successful life, may create confusion and conflict. His achieving deeper meditations, at the expense of spending time working, will be a source of anger, as you battle to achieve the cash to buy the home you've always dreamed of owning.

The more you deem that your idea of success constitutes "Success," while your partner's concept is wrong or not really success, you create polarisation. It's natural then that if your idea of success is financial gain, you will seek a person who has no such desire, in order to balance yourself.

"While I'm meditating, he is flying around the world on business making serious money," commented one woman. "Our worlds are just too far apart for the relationship to work. He doesn't get me and I don't understand him."

While Grace worked extremely hard to achieve a good income, (which made her feel secure,) her husband's idea of success meant taking time out to go to the gym, to go fishing regularly and to work at a pace that did not burn him out.

Half of you reading this will relate to her and what she was doing to achieve happiness and the other half to him. Both groups will feel that they are absolutely right in their choice. The difference though, is that she saw happiness as a goal, while he saw it as a state of being. While it remained a goal for her she felt she had to work hard to achieve it, because in her history that's what it meant to achieve a goal. While for him, the opposite was true. His happiness was achieved by not doing. By having the discipline to enjoy all that is, as opposed to all that might be.

Healing

Identify what success means to you and allow that to be your guide. Remember that if everything in the universe is perfect, then there can be no failure or lack of success.

Every step that appears to be going backward, is in fact simply building momentum to move forward.

Acknowledging what both your aspirations are. Don't judge each other - rather come to accept each as different but not better. Trying to make the other person have the same goal as you is not realistic and designed to make them feel a failure even when in their mind they are achieving their way not yours. The joy at winning a sporting goal will not be judged against the other's ability to become a M.D. Both people can simply enjoy the success of the other, encourage their pursuits and have mutual respect for each other's successes.

Chapter Fifteen

The Damsel in Distress and the Knight in a Shining BMW

- It's late, she has some typing still to complete; he offers to stay with her until she's finished and walk her to the station.
- The company profits are diminishing, jobs are on the line and she comes up with a plan to rescue the situation.
- She has a puncture; over 50 motorists ignore her attempts to change tyres, until he stops to help.
- She is going through a very difficult divorce and it's his guidance and support that get her through the trying times.

Enter the heroine.

The classic fairytale archetypes of the Heroine and Hero/Knight, reappear in our everyday lives in the guise of leaders of organisations dedicated to the aid and upliftment of others, saving the rainforests or assisting endangered species.

Archetypes are not always faithful to the gender they describe; so a Knight may be a woman, and the Damsel in Distress (the person being "saved,") may be a man. The words just describe the type of energy between the two, which corresponds to the archetypes describing that energy.

In our own personal relationships they can lift us up out of troublesome situations, slaying the proverbial dragon in the form of an abusive relationship, loneliness, lack of self worth or any other situation that has kept us in distress. This is the story of the woman who is walking down the road with her two small children, fleeing an abusive marriage and a poverty stricken situation and who gets picked up and offered a lift by a man who just happens to be a multi-millionaire and who takes her under his wing and offers her and her children, a life they could only ever have dreamt of.

If there is a crisis, the Knight appears. What then can be the harm in this you may ask? Surely we need as many Knights as we can find on this planet? The answer is yes, unless the hero/ine works in the shadow side of the hero, becoming the archetype of the Rescuer.

The Rescuer needs to rescue in order to validate their self-worth. The more they rescue, the better about themselves they come to feel. It may be stray dogs, abandoned children or men with addiction problems, but whenever the Knight sees a pattern emerging that indicates the rescue is based on the need for improving self worth, it's an indication that the Knight is in fact a shadow Knight or Rescuer.

A bit of self worth boosting though is not the problem. The problem is that the Rescuer needs to rescue to the point that it does not serve them or the person they are rescuing to heal. They need to be rescuing because this makes them feel needed. If the person they are rescuing shows signs of rehabilitation or recovery in any way, this leaves the Rescuer without a role. There is also the belief from the Rescuer, that what is in actual fact help, can be mistaken for intimacy – the belief that because they have rescued a person, somehow that person now owes them intimacy and a relationship. In many so called "healing," fields shadow rescuers can be found. Those who have set out to help and to heal, yet this is a mirror for the help and healing they themselves need.

Rose was an alternative practitioner. She was devoted to her work and clients. Boundaries did not exist and clients were able to call at any time of the day or night to ask Rose to help them through whatever crisis had occurred. Some saw this as selfless devotion, yet when Rose started burning out the warning signs were flashing that her relationships with her clients were not in balance. Helping clients had become a way of avoiding helping herself. In other words she had taken her need for help and projected onto others, leaving her feeling needy, and if she admitted it resentful. Many therapists do this. They subconsciously recognise the need for help in healing their own wounds and project this as a need to help others, while often ignoring their own needs. As they say: "metaphysician heal thyself."

Women are particularly prevalent when it comes to Rescuing energy. We want to help our children, rescue our family members and put our partners onto the straight and narrow, to avoid them having to experience pain.

Kirsty had a husband who was a cocaine addict. She loved the man dearly, but the roller coaster ride that comes with living with an addict was proving too much for her to cope with. Somewhere between his up days and his withdrawal induced down days, she could capture a little bit of their previous relationship. Costly drug rehabilitation programmes had failed, counselling and other support programmes had not improved the situation. Looking back into her past, Kirtsy could identify a pattern of substance abuse: her father had been an alcoholic. She had been engaged to another man with alcohol dependency and after that relationship had ended, she had married her present partner. From the age of a small child, Kirsty had believed that somehow she was responsible for getting her dad well - a belief that she had carried into her marriage, now in relation to her husband. This pattern is typical of a Rescuer.

Not all Knights/Rescuers lives revolve around rescuing those with substance addictions. Rescuing can be related to rescuing women with a history of depression, abuse or insecurity. Or rescuing can relate to impoverished people, stray dogs or abandoned babies. Now obviously this is not to say that all those giving help in the world are just externalising their own need for care, however it can be a factor in some cases, where people will volunteer their services as a way of confirming to themselves what good people they are, when their subconscious might be hinting that there are demons lurking which they would rather avoid.

One woman I knew, sobbed uncontrollably for days, over the loss of a wild baby bird she had picked up a few days before. Now, its not that the loss of an animal doesn't warrant upset, (I adore my animals and will be very sad when they pass on), but this was way out of proportion and went on for a lot longer than would be considered normal grief. In feeling so deeply for the loss of the bird, this Rescuer was in some way crying for her own life. The bird was her, and in its death, she related to the part of her, the small, frail, lonely part of her, that had been abandoned and made her feel as if she was dying.

Cecil and Fay, were married with four children, yet they found the time to help out at the local childcare. They became so involved and devoted so much time and energy that everyone commented on their selfless efforts. At home though, it was a different story, as one of their children was to tell me years later. They, as the children of these "saints," felt completely neglected and rejected and all suffered as a consequence. The parents had actually had a very unhappy relationship and escaping from home became a way of avoiding having to deal with these issues. Different people meeting them in their different roles then, would have very different viewpoints. To some they were Heroes while to others they were people who desperately needed to rescue their own relationship and their own children.

The payoff for the Rescuer

So why does the Rescuer rescue? Simply because by rescuing he or she validates their self worth. Those rescued feel grateful and feeling the gratitude of others feels good. Rescuers need to feel needed.

In my book *The girl who bites her nails and the man who is always late*, I write about Animal Hoarding as a habit. The psychological disorder where (usually elderly spinsters) "save" animals only to treat them horrifically. They want the accolades from society for their good deeds, rather than genuine concern for the animals in their care.

Rescuing is also as mentioned, a projection of our own need for help, which is why the majority of Rescuers are deep down resentful to those they rescue for not helping them, even though this is not what they project.

The Payoff for the Damsel in Distress

For the Damsel in Distress, being rescued is a way of stepping into a Child archetype and not having to own responsibility for their own healing. Help me, help me, is easier to say than: Help me to help myself.

To help ourselves means to have to own responsibility for our lives. That's pretty hard to do – it's much easier to swoon into the arms of a willing Knight.

Healing the Knight and the Damsel in Distress

To heal the Rescuer, is to heal our own craving to be needed by others. To do so is to realise that we don't need others to be ok with who we are. Simply being is all we need be. We also need to recognise our own projected needs onto those who we wish to save. And rather than save them, look first at saving ourselves. Then we can work through the enlightened Hero, to work more effectively in healing those in need.

To heal the Damsel, requires that the Damsel assume responsibility for his/her own healing, rather than rely on others. To rely on others, is to hand over ones power to them. I am always struck in western medicine how much power we hand over to the medical fraternity, even when we know that many errors of judgments have been made and that many medications have been proven not to be quite so miraculous as originally believed when side-effects are taken into account. If you simply take all that is said to you without doing your own research and trusting your own inner guidance, like the Damsel, you risk losing your personal power and handing it to someone who may be developed enough to honour you, but who may equally not be.

As the Damsel, learn to claim your power. Step into your own shoes. Knowledge is power. Become responsible for who you are and your life. Rescue yourself.

Chapter Sixteen

Transmuting duality

What's wrong with being right?

Life and relationships are seldom easy.

They may have moments, (for some extended periods) of intense pleasure and joy, yet around each corner we constantly are made to face new difficulties – irrespective as to whether we are Americans, Africans, Asian, Europeans or any other culture. Whether we are rich or poor, educated or illiterate, attractive or less so, strong physically or weak, life is a giant school, where learning through experience is often the only way we can graduate to higher levels of awareness. Living in the expectation that life and relationships should be easy, is setting ourselves up for inevitable disappointment. Accepting that life is not always the way we would like it to be, but perfect nevertheless, makes us more able to accept the challenge the experience offers.

What we may believe is "right" may not be so. Our attachment to this belief will only cause us hardship and pain. Jason has left Miranda. They have two children. He, by her account, is wrong. He does feel guilt for leaving her, but was finding the relationship intolerable to the point that it was making him physically (life threateningly so) ill. Marriage guidance had not improved the situation. Was he wrong or right? What if he was neither? What if they were acting out a dance of energy, as their souls attempted to bring them into balance?

The longer Miranda holds onto the belief that Jason was "wrong," and she was "right," the longer she will remain in pain and anger, and cause herself more suffering.

Your relationship is there to test you. To allow you to work through your issues and in teaching you to love yourself, to learn to simultaneously love the other. If you reject the potential learning: - if you expect to reach graduation before you've passed grade one, you will be disappointed, confused and disillusioned. If however you accept the challenge – and see that for every up, there will be a down and affirm to yourself that being easy would not facilitate your personal growth, you can reach deep into yourself to find the courage to work with issues, as opposed to avoiding them or spiral down into naming and blaming.

It's not easy. If it were, we'd all be in blissful, harmonious relationships the whole time. And very few people are. Accept that you are here to learn. To evolve is not for woosies! The fact though that you are reading this book, is an indication that there is a part of you that acknowledges that you want more – more love, more intimacy, more acceptance. Problem is, we all would like it to drop into our laps from our partner (while they probably feel the same way)."Be," as Ghandi said, "the change you want to see in the world."

My mother was a marriage guidance counsellor. Whenever she saw one party in the relationship, listening to their side of the story, it was hard not to believe that they were totally right. However, when speaking to the other partner, the same story would emerge, albeit from a completely different perspective. And she would see that neither was the Truth but only true from their perspectives.

As St Paul said in Corinthians 1: "For now we see through a glass, darkly..." In other words our viewpoint is tinted or tainted by our life's experiences. The clearer we become the clearer our viewpoint is. In the newer versions of the bible, it is sometimes translated as: "For now we see in a mirror, dimly…" So from this we can see that the world is mirrored to us, dimmed through our own experiences.

By recognising that the universe is one large balance seeking mechanism – one paradox of opposites, you can start to work with duality. You can begin to identify your projections, see the history from where they came, and work towards transcending them. If the critical Parent lurks within you, see ancestrally where it came from. Forget about judging it. That will only result in guilt, which will hold you in the past. The truth is we all have shadow sides – aspects of ourselves that we may feel are not pleasant. By avoiding them and attempting to suppress them you give them power. By acknowledging them and accepting them you bring them from the dark to the light and transcend their existence.

If a person were to claim great religious convictions and profess that her/his beliefs are "right," yet at the same time have intense mood swings, for example, going from being demure and overtly sweet, to harshly criticising and demeaning, is this person balanced? Clearly not so. In making herself/himself so right and everyone else so wrong, she/he has put themselves out of balance. If her actions show that she is swinging from one side of herself to the other, surely she has a way to go to be centred? To the degree that we are balanced, have inner contentment, have personal integrity and to the degree that we have a conscience, is a better mark of our evolvement than what belief system we follow.

By reading this book, you have started a journey, or moved further along the road of self-discovery. As you work through the issues discussed in the book, others may not initially notice the difference in you. As you seek to embrace and then transmute these archetypal aspects of yourself, you'll know and experience the realisation that: "as I change so the world around me changes."

It does not matter whether you have identified yourself as a critical Parent, a Tyrant or a Rebel. Ultimately I believe we experience all archetypes. Feeling "less than," as a result or judging one as worse or better, serves absolutely no purpose but to stop your developing into a happier more balanced person. Accept with love the person you are, and all the events and people that have led up to your being who you are. Now you have the opportunity to release what no longer serves you.

You are not wrong to be a Tyrant or right to be a Child, anymore than the wind is right to be the wind, while the earth is wrong not to be the water. That thinking holds you in duality. Accept your own shadow archetypes and it will make it easier to accept those of others. At the point of doing so you move beyond their duality.

Caroline Myss once said in a workshop, that for everyone of the audience sitting there wanting to release a past bad relationship experience, there were an equal amount of their partners sitting somewhere else wanting to release them. In truth if one person suffers in a relationship, the other usually does to.

Developing communication

Open, honest communication is essential to an interdependent relationship. How do you achieve this?

Let's say you are feeling unheard by your partner. You feel they don't understand you and this has become a serious issue for you. The common way of approaching the subject may be:

"Look, I'm tired of you being emotionally withdrawn. I find you an unfeeling bastard/bitch and I'm sick of it."

Now you have attacked your partner. Their response will either be to retaliate or withdraw. Neither of which is going to lead to better communication.

If on the other hand you drop the need to accuse them but simply express your own feelings, you will create a better possibility of being understood. It's also important to get your partner's buy-in to what you are about to say as that way they have entered into the conversation willingly/by their own choice.

"May I share something with you?" you may start off by saying. If your partner agrees then this becomes a mutual discussion, not your personal unsolicited dumping ground of emotions.

Bringing it back to yourself, as opposed to being accusatory; you might say: "I have been feeling that you have been withdrawing from me. This is upsetting for me, as I really want a relationship where I can share my feelings with the person I love. My feelings are important to me and consequently it means a lot to me to have them recognised."

Now you have openly and honestly communicated how YOU feel. Can you see now that not having been made to be wrong in the relationship, you have opened up the doorway of authentic communication? Chances are your partner may respond honestly now along the lines of: "gee, I didn't realise that it meant so much to you," or "I guess I have been rather caught up in my own stuff recently, do you want to share some of these feelings with me now?"

I have found with this approach that it is possible to say things to people without any adverse reaction that otherwise may have caused huge conflict. The secret is that when you drop attacking or making the other person wrong, you move into a heart-based form of communication, as opposed to an ego based communication. The other person senses that you are speaking from the heart and responds similarly. The ego based communication is always destructive, while the heart-based communication is always constructive, compassionate and done with infinite love and understanding of your own and your partner's imbalances.

Going backwards to go forwards.

Be aware though, that when we have spent our lives being a certain way, the path is well worn. As we walk the new path, all may seem well until a crisis occurs (which it inevitably does!) Instantly we can slip back into old ways of being. The difference is that we are now conscious of what is happening, and we can sit back, examine the situation, even laugh at ourselves and in our realisation make the decision to change.

Perhaps spend some time each day alone, reflecting on where you may have been out of balance. Look to understand why. Ask your inner self for ways to move beyond this behaviour.

Remember though that life is, as they say a journey rather than a destination. Enjoy the work/journey. Let go of the need to achieve the goal. You and your world are evolving so the goal is not statistically waiting to be achieved. You are constantly then a "work in progress." If you are like most of us you'll slip back. Acknowledge the fact, smile, be grateful that you can see the experience for what it is, let it go and pick yourself up and continue. "The gold," as a shaman once said to me, "is in the journey not at the end of it." A rainbow shows us this. The mythical pot of gold is not at the end of the rainbow, but in the journey we take to find it.

Tools we need for a healthy relationship with ourselves and others:

- **Self-esteem.** If you have a healthy sense of self-esteem, you will attract like-minded others. You will also believe that you deserve a interdependent relationship.
- **Purpose.** The ability to know what it is we want out of life. If you have no goal what are you aiming for? No aim, no gain! Share your vision and use it to inspire others.
- **Self respect and unconditional love.** You will attract who you are. This means we have to start on a path of self-love, self-trust and acceptance if we are to attract a similar partner. If we don't value ourselves, why should our partner?
- **Choice.** The ability to be governed by our own choices and not doing what we think will simply please others or win their approval.
- **Honour.** The ability to honour your own vision and your partner's.
- **Wholeness.** You are a person in your own right – you do not need a relationship to feel whole.
- **Truth.** The ability to be true to yourself even if it does not win the approval of others. The ability to always live in your integrity. Your word is your truth. This inspires others to trust you. Trust leads to having respect for yourself and your partner. From this then we create the space for intimacy. You cannot have intimacy without trust and truth. You cannot have self respect and thus self-esteem without being true to yourself. Are you prepared to hold onto a relationship at the expense of your own sense of self? Realise then that to have truth involves the risk of losing your relationship, should the other person not be able to honour your truth. Then you have to question if the relationship is worth having if to have it involves not being truthful, loosing your self respect and not having intimacy.
- **Communication and expression.** Open and honest communication with your own inner self and with others. Express who you are and what you feel.
- **Judgement**. Release the need for it in your life. Both of self-judgement and the judgement of others.
- **Present.** Be present. Let go of the past and the need to blame. Let go of the future and the fear of what may come. Unless you are present you can't be intimate.
- **Perfectionism**. Let go of the need for everything to be right. Be flexible accept that your version of right may not be THE version. Remember either everything in the universe is perfect the way it is or nothing is. Perfectionism cannot have degrees.

- **Flexibility.** Let go of the need to control and dominate.
- **Forgiveness.** Learn to forgive yourself and others and move on – the quicker the better. Asking for forgiveness empowers the other person far more than simply saying sorry. Through humbling ourselves we become more empowered and we empower others. That's what makes for a great human being and great relationships.
- **The ability to say thank-you.** Realise how awesome this universe is. Make a daily practise of thanking your partner and appreciating all they do and bring to your world. Don't take them or anything else in your life for granted. The more grateful you are the more the universe opens up to give you more to be grateful for.
- **Learn to recognise when your imbalances are projecting into opposing archetypes.** Then you have the tools by now, to actively move closer into the centre of the see-saw of your relationship, rather than further apart.

Foregoing forgiveness.

Initially it may be hard to be grateful to the Tyrant who has made your life miserable. Thanking them for the role they have played in your life may be unthinkable. Yet once we see that this very Tyrant was the person we most needed to balance our Victim, at this point in our lives, we can be grateful to them for the role they have played in bringing us to this point of better balance.

Likewise, if we are married to a Child, we can see that in their inability to assume responsibility, we have learnt a huge amount, through having to assume greater responsibility ourselves. In putting the pieces of the puzzle together they become not the absolute wrong person for us, but completely the right person to do the job that our souls required of them. The enemy then becomes the greatest friend.

Spend time exploring these possibilities. Start thanking the Universe for this person and the role they have or perhaps are still playing. There are no exceptions. You did not just get unlucky. Also then see the wondrousness of how in changing yourself, you know the world and your relationships will change. It's up to you.

When you reach the point that you can honour the role that your partner has played in your life you can then see that there is actually nothing to forgive them for. Forgiveness, by implication, means that someone must be wrong (and another right). At this point you get back the energy that you had given to your anger/resentment etc and so in letting them go, you get the reward of becoming more empowered.

What if there was no wrong or right? Just two souls playing roles to assist each others' development?

Think back on your life. Wasn't it more often that the people who appeared to have harmed you, were the trigger for your own personal growth? Through them, you found strength you never knew existed. Through them, you made the decision that changed your life. They were the actor/ess you needed in your own true life drama. Hold them in your heart and honour them for the awesome role they have played in your life.

A reporter who was interviewing me, told me her husband died, leaving their financial affairs in a sorry state. At the age of 62, she travelled on her own to China and taught in a remote part.. She could have remained at home feeling angry towards her husband for the lack of finances. Instead she reached within herself and found the courage to take her life in an altogether different direction. In China life was a matter of day to day survival. "Having to literally live from one moment to the next, brought me into present time, where there was no space for past regrets or future worries. I felt if I could survive that year, far away from everyone and anything familiar in a place where I knew no-one and couldn't speak the language, I could survive anything. By being forced to live in the present, I was far more relaxed. When I look back on that year, I can remember almost every moment of it, whereas back at home now, each day blurs into the next and I find it hard to remember even what I did last week." The experience had altered her perspective on life completely allowing her to move beyond blame and the restrictive energy of feeling a Victim.

In Summary

There are many more archetypal pairs than those included in the book - the amount is almost limitless. However, the principle of seeking balance through opposites is constant.

There has been some talk in so called "New Age" circles that we are moving into an age where opposites are no longer valid. I cannot subscribe to this idea, while we live in a world of opposites: Day/night. Light/dark. Good/evil. Male/female Black/white. Up/down. North/south. East/west. Positive/negative. Tall/short. Old/new. Rich/poor. etc. Duality is the nature of our world and we express this through our relationships. We came from The One. Then we were divided, as in the story of Adam and Eve. Now we want to become whole again. Only when we transcend this duality can we move to the realm of the whole and holy. To do this, we need to work at becoming one within ourselves. Then the relationship to ourselves, will be mirrored in the relationships we have externally.

My encouragement to you would be to let go of blame, both towards yourself and others. Start working at viewing your relationships through archetypal eyes. When you see the see-saw in action, make a conscious decision to love and accept your partner's archetype and its mirror in yourself. Move into the point of balance on your see-saw and watch your world through new, enlightened eyes.

This is when you discover there is no Mr. Wrong or Mr. Right, (or Ms. Wrong /Ms. Right). Only yourself as part of the Universe in this enormously dynamic and exciting game of *be*ing.

Bibliography

Berne, Eric, *Games People Play,* Grove Press, New York, 1963

Gadd, Ann, *Climbing the Beanstalk,* Findhorn Press, Scotland 2007

Gadd, Ann, *The Girl Who Bites Her Nails And The Man Who Is Always Late*, Findhorn Press, Scotland, 2007

Ulsamer Bertold and Beaumont Colleen, *Art and Practice of Family Constellations: Leading Family Constellations as Developed by Bert Hellinger,*Berlin, *2003*

Lipton, Bruce, Ph.D *The Biology of Belief,* Mountain of Love, California, 2005

Myss, Caroline, Ph.D, *Why People Don't Heal And How They Can*, Bantam, London, 1997